W0043154

PORTFOLIO

THREE MERCHANTS OF BOMBAY

LAKSHMI SUBRAMANIAN is professor of history at the Centre for Studies in Social Sciences, Calcutta. She has a PhD from Visva-Bharati (Santiniketan) and has previously taught at Jamia Millia Islamia, New Delhi, the University of Calcutta and Visva-Bharati.

GURCHARAN DAS is a world-renowned author, commentator and public intellectual. His bestselling books include *India Unbound*, *The Difficulty of Being Good* and *India Grows at Night*. His other literary works consist of a novel, *A Fine Family*, a book of essays, *The Elephant Paradigm*, and an anthology, *Three Plays*. A graduate of Harvard University, Das was CEO of Procter & Gamble, India, before he took early retirement to become a full-time writer. He lives in Delhi.

THE STORY OF INDIAN BUSINESS
Series Editor: Gurcharan Das

Arthashastra: The Science of Wealth by Thomas R. Trautmann

The World of the Tamil Merchant: Pioneers of International Trade by Kanakalatha Mukund

The Mouse Merchant: Money in Ancient India by Arshia Sattar

The East India Company: The World's Most Powerful Corporation by Tirthankar Roy

Caravans: Punjabi Khatri Merchants on the Silk Road by Scott C. Levi

Globalization before Its Time: The Gujarati Merchants from Kachchh by Chhaya Goswami (edited by Jaithirth Rao)

Three Merchants of Bombay: Business Pioneers of the Nineteenth Century by Lakshmi Subramanian

The Marwaris: From Jagat Seth to the Birlas by Thomas A. Timberg

Goras and Desis: Managing Agencies and the Making of Corporate India by Omkar Goswami

Indian Railways: Weaving of a National Tapestry by Bibek Debroy, Sanjay Chadha, Vidya Krishnamurthi

THE STORY OF INDIAN BUSINESS

THREE MERCHANTS OF BOMBAY

Business Pioneers of the Nineteenth Century

LAKSHMI SUBRAMANIAN

Introduction by
Gurcharan Das

PORTFOLIO
PENGUIN

An imprint of Penguin Random House

PORTFOLIO

USA | Canada | UK | Ireland | Australia
New Zealand | India | South Africa | China | Singapore

Portfolio is part of the Penguin Random House group of companies
whose addresses can be found at global.penguinrandomhouse.com

Published by Penguin Random House India Pvt. Ltd
4th Floor, Capital Tower 1, MG Road,
Gurugram 122 002, Haryana, India

Penguin
Random House
India

First published as *Three Merchants of Bombay: Doing Business in
Times of Change* in Allen Lane by Penguin Books India 2012
Published under the present title in Portfolio 2016

Copyright © Lakshmi Subramanian 2012
Introduction copyright © Gurcharan Das 2012

All rights reserved

10 9 8 7 6 5 4 3 2

The views and opinions expressed in this book are the author's own and the
facts are as reported by her which have been verified to the extent possible, and
the publishers are not in any way liable for the same.

ISBN 9780143426196

Typeset in Aldine401 BT by SŪRYA, New Delhi
Printed at Manipal Technologies Limited, India

This book is sold subject to the condition that it shall not, by way of trade
or otherwise, be lent, resold, hired out, or otherwise circulated without the
publisher's prior consent in any form of binding or cover other than that in
which it is published and without a similar condition including this condition
being imposed on the subsequent purchaser.

www.penguin.co.in

MIX
Paper | Supporting
responsible forestry
FSC® C043100

This is a legitimate digitally printed version of the book and therefore might not
have certain extra finishing on the cover.

CONTENTS

Introduction by Gurcharan Das   vii

Author's Note   xxvii

Chronology   xxxi

Prologue   xxxiii

1. Merchants and Rulers in the Interstices of Empire 1

2. Trawadi Arjunji Nathji: The 'Honourable 47
   Company's Shroff'

3. Jamsetjee Jeejeebhoy: The First Parsi Baronet 88

4. Premchand Roychand: A Man for All Seasons 144

   Epilogue: The Romance of Commerce 195

   Notes   211

   Bibliography   232

INTRODUCTION

THE CRAVING FOR adventure and the love of profit are inherent in human nature. Hence they say exchange is natural and all-pervasive. But then, why does the commercial spirit flower in some places and at certain times, and not in others? Lakshmi Subramanian has narrated here, with elegance, the stories of three legendary merchant princes—Trawadi Arjunji Nathji, Jamsetjee Jeejeebhoy and Premchand Roychand. In doing so she has breathed life into the business world of western India in the latter half of the eighteenth and the first half of the nineteenth centuries—a most unlikely time for the rise of 'animal spirits' in the disturbed, lawless 'period of transition' between the decline of the Mughal empire and the rise of the British Raj.

The relationship between commerce and the rise of cities and prosperity is an exciting tale that goes back in time to when the city first emerged in human history. It also goes to the heart of the question of wealth and poverty of nations— why some grow rich and others remain poor. These are the sort of questions that engage our unique multi-volume history of Indian business.

The Story of Indian Business

Three Merchants of Bombay is the fourth book in Penguin's *The Story of Indian Business*. The series seeks to unearth great ideas in business and economics that have shaped commerce in the Indian subcontinent while entertaining us with the romance of the high seas and the adventure in the bazaars. Leading contemporary scholars closely examine, in this series, historical texts, inscriptions and records, and interpret them in a lively, sharp and authoritative manner for the intelligent reader who may not have prior background in the field. Each slender volume offers an enduring perspective on business enterprise in the past, avoiding the pitfalls of simplistically cataloguing a set of lessons for today. The value of the exercise, if we are successful, will be to promote in the reader, a long-term sensibility which can help to understand the material bases for our present human condition and to think sensibly about our economic future. Taken together, the series as a whole celebrates the ideal captured in the Sanskrit word *artha* meaning material well-being, which was one of the aims of classical Indian life.

The first three books were published in early 2012. The series began with Tom Trautman's sparkling interpretation for our times of the renowned treatise on the science of wealth, *Arthashastra*, which was authored over 2000 years ago and is considered the world's first manual on political economy. Our second work, Tirthankar Roy's radiant account of the English East India Company, taught us, among other things, how much the modern multinational corporation is a child of the much-reviled Company. In the third book,

Kanakalatha Mukund took us into the beguiling world of Tamil merchants, whose lives she drew from the epics, *Silappadikaram* and *Manimekalai* and other historical materials, up to the end of the Chola empire.

Following these books lies a veritable feast—three more books shall cover the ancient and early medieval periods: Gregory Schopen presents the *Business Model of Early Buddhist Monasticism* based on the *Mulasarvastivada-vinaya*; Himanshu Prabha Ray takes us into the maritime trading world of the western-Indian Ocean, along the Kanara and Gujarat coasts, using the Gujarati translation of the Sanskrit work, *Lekhapaddhati*; and Arshia Sattar recounts the brilliant adventures based on *Kathasaritsagara* and other sources in *The Mouse Merchant* among other tales. Then Scott Levi takes off from the early modern period to the modern one with the over 500-year-old saga of Multani traders in their caravans travelling through central Asia, rooted in the works of Zia al-Din Barani's *Tarikh-i-Firuz Shahi* and Jean-Baptiste Tavernier. Furthermore, the celebrated Sanjay Subrahmanyam and Muzaffar Alam transport us into the world of sultans, shopkeepers and portfolio-capitalists in Mughal India, while Ishan Chakrabarti traces the ethically individualistic world of Banarsidas, a Jain merchant in Mughal times via his diary *Ardhakathanak*.

The feast doesn't end there. Chhaya Goswami dives deep into the Indian Ocean to recount the tale of Kachchhi enterprise in the triangle of Zanzibar, Muscat and Mandvi from 1750 to 1900. Tom Timberg revisits the bold, risk-taking world of the Marwaris, and Raman Mahadevan describes Nattukottai Chettiars' search for fortune. Then, Vikramjit Banerjee presents, through the works of Gandhi, Vivekananda, Nehru, Ambedkar and others, the competing visions of prosperity among the men who fought for India's freedom in the early twentieth century. Finally, Medha Kudaisiya rounds up the series by breathing life into the debates surrounding the *Bombay Plan*, drawn by eminent industrialists in 1944–45 who wrestled with the proper roles of the public and private sectors.

The privilege of reading these rich and diverse volumes has left me—one reader—with a sense of wonder at the vivid, dynamic and illustrious role played by trade and economic enterprise in advancing Indian civilization.

The Importance of Being Bombay

Lakshmi Subramanian's three masterly biographical portraits raise many intriguing questions, and in this introduction I shall explore one of them: the relationship between the growth of commerce, the rise of cities, and the rule of law. Which comes first? Do cities grow because they offer peace and the rule of law to merchants? Or is it the other way around? Does the growth in commerce create the resources for investing in better institutions of security, law and order? The rise of Bombay and the decline of Surat in western India in the 100 years between 1750 and 1850 is a good laboratory in which to examine these questions.

Charles II, king of England, received Bombay as dowry on his marriage to the Portuguese princess Catharine of Braganza in June 1661. More than a hundred years later, the original seven islets were still a 'dreary settlement resembling the backwaters that flowed' into it, according to our author. Then it rose spectacularly and went on to become the financial capital of India. How did this come to be, especially in the troubled and warlike conditions of the eighteenth century—after the collapse of the Mughal authority, the rise of the formidable Marathas, and the growth of English power?

The island city rose after the decline of Surat because it offered a competitive advantage in governance. When the opportunity came by way of external stimuli from the global economy, the 'dreary settlement' responded. Bombay offered the classical conditions of peace, security, and the rule of law, and it did this far better than its competitors. No one has expressed this better than its first Governor, Gerald Aungier, when he promised Bombay's inhabitants 'equality before the law' and 'justice without fear, favour, in respect of persons'. In a moving speech quoted by Mariam Dossal in *Theatre of Conflict, City of Hope: Mumbai 1660 to Present Times*, Aungier gave this advice to the first judge appointed in Bombay in 1672:

> The inhabitants of this Island consist of several Nations and Religions to wit—English, Portuguese and other Christians, Moores, and Jentue, but you, when you sit in this seat of Justice and Judgement, must looke upon them with one single eye as I doe, without distinction of Nation or Religion, for they ... have all an equal title and right to Justice and you must doe them all Justice, even the meanest person of the Island, and in

particular the Poore, the Orphan, the Widow and the stranger . . .

Bombay also offered a great natural harbour with miles upon miles of deep, sheltered water, perfect for big ships. It had a vigorous naval police to safeguard commercial vessels from pirates on the high seas. It had the Mayor's Court, which enforced contracts between merchants of all races. The traditional Indian Bania appreciated the British conception of individual legal responsibility, which limited his financial liability only to himself and his lifetime, as against the traditional Indian norm that an individual's debt had to be made good by the joint family and the liability extended over generations.

Until the post-Mughal regional kingdoms stabilized the wandering life of a merchant entailed risks of every kind. Pillage was not an unusual means of existence. Hence the merchant sought the protection of a city. But the island city offered much more. It had an open and trusting environment which welcomed all types of business people. It protected private property and confiscated it only in the rarest circumstances. It did not suffer from the Mughal landed gentry's disdain of the merchant nor from the contemptuous attitude of British Calcutta's 'burra sahib'.

Hence Banias from commercial centres all over western India began to stream into the island, bringing with them an abundance of entrepreneurial dynamism. Soon Bombay was making room for Parsi ship- and dock-builders, legendary Gujarati men of trade, Jain shroffs, Marwari bankers, Konkani Muslim traders, Baghdadi Jews and European free-traders.

As a result it acquired its peculiarly cosmopolitan character early on. The relatively smaller presence of the British official community made it less hierarchical and less racist than Calcutta. Anyone could rise to the top as long as he had what it took. The stories of Jamsetjee Jeejeebhoy and Premchand Roychand are testament to this.

The Banias also brought with them their traditional institutions and networks, which proved useful when it came to brokering the cotton business between the fields in south Gujarat and Kathiawar and the port of Bombay. The *hundi*, the legendary financial instrument in particular was indispensable in financing the business between the port and mofussil cotton areas, which had their own currencies and byzantine exchange rates. The hundi became the common currency, and shroffs, such as the renowned Motishaw, Bansilal Abhirchand, Kaka Shah and others in Bazaar Gate, became powerful bankers. To the hundi they added other financial instruments such as 'respondentia', a risk-sharing mechanism in maritime trade which helped to reduce the hazard in 'consignment trade'.

Because the early merchant princes went on to become generous philanthropists who made a visible impact on public culture, the island city acquired a modern atmosphere. Public philanthropy brought respectability to commerce and dignity to the bourgeoisie, as our author explains in some detail. All these qualities go a long way in explaining Bombay's success. But the big stimulus which lifted the island city on to the world stage came from the outside. Bombay became part of a global trading network in the late eighteenth and early nineteenth centuries.

'Indian Opium for the Chinese, Chinese Tea for the Britons, and British Raj for the Indians'

Bombay became a critical link in satisfying the insatiable appetite of the English for tea, and of the Chinese for opium. After William Pitt (the Elder) lowered import duties on Chinese tea in 1784 the demand from English households exploded. Soon millions of pounds worth of tea began to travel on the ships of the Company from Canton to the British ports. On the return journey these ships picked up silver to pay for the tea. The huge drain of silver, however, created a serious balance-of-payments problem for Britain.

The Chinese were not interested in exchanging their tea for British-made goods, but they were attracted to two things that India produced—cotton and opium. Soon ships began to ply between Bombay and Canton filled with cotton from Gujarat and opium from Malwa in Madhya Pradesh (and more significantly, opium grown in Bihar, under the supervision of the Company, which left for China via Calcutta). The British began to balance the trade by paying for the tea with cotton and opium, and this solved their balance-of-payments problem.

Thus a bustling triangular trade developed among India, China and Europe, in which private traders played an increasingly important role, as the monopoly of the Company broke. The London–Canton trade had always been a Company monopoly, but the Bombay–Canton trade had mostly been private. Private traders and agency houses engaged vigorously in shipping, financing, underwriting and the remittance of funds. In the opium trade the Parsi community played a crucial role as shippers and consignment merchants, and its most celebrated member was, of course, Jamsetjee Jeejeebhoy, whose partnership with the agency house of Jardine Matheson and Company propelled him to the top. Tan Chung (whom Lakshmi Subramanian quotes) summed up this triangular trade nicely: 'Indian opium for the Chinese, English tea for the Britons, and British Raj for the Indians.'

Abraham Lincoln and Premchand Roychand

The Opium Wars between Britain and China after the 1840s dampened the growth prospects of the opium trade. But the rise of Bombay was not to be stopped. An event, thousands of miles away on the American continent, brought forth the next stimulus to the city's development. President Abraham Lincoln's abolition of slavery in America led to the American Civil War in the 1860s and abruptly cut off the supply of cotton from the Southern United States to the mills of Lancashire. On this occasion it was an enterprising Gujarati cotton merchant, Premchand Roychand, who sensed the opportunity of a lifetime as cotton prices skyrocketed. He stepped into the vacuum and encouraged Gujarat's cotton farmers to plant the new variety that the English mills needed.

Farmers everywhere are creatures of habit and do not value novelty the way merchants do. But the Gujarati farmers responded quickly and brilliantly. Within months Indian cotton had replaced American cotton. The cotton boom brought in a colossal amount of capital to Bombay. Fortunes were made overnight and speculation in cotton futures became a way of life. Even paan-wallahs on street corners were caught in the frenzy. The surplus wealth soon found another outlet—private companies began to finance the reclamation of land from the sea—and this laid the foundations of a truly modern city. If Jeejeebhoy was the top dog of the opium trade, Premchand Roychand, an Oswal Jain, became the 'king of cotton'. He also manipulated the Bank of Bombay to his advantage and helped finance the reclamation programme.

The bubble could not last. The American Civil War came to an end in 1865. The supply of American cotton to Lancashire resumed, and Lancashire preferred it to Bombay's—not least because of the much shorter journey across the Atlantic. The Suez Canal was only built in 1870, but even after that, Bombay's bales would have had to make a longer journey to Manchester. An extraordinary degree of panic gripped the city of Bombay as the cotton market crashed. Huge fortunes were lost overnight. Our author describes it vividly:

> Gripped by a situation of unprecedented panic, the city went berserk as investors rushed to dispose of their shares in the bubble companies—but there were no buyers. The banks and financial companies that had advanced them the funds found themselves in a hopeless situation. Tumbling prices, panicky investors and depleted banks embodied the crisis that the city experienced; and predictably enough, the edifice built

on shares and stocks and bubble companies collapsed
like a house of cards.

Premchand Roychand lost a fortune, and Lakshmi
Subramanian describes vividly that the same man who could
manipulate the Bank of Bombay, showed character in
adversity as he made good his debts as well as the debts of
others who were associated with him. This thought is worth
pondering over as one passes by the magnificent neo-Gothic
Rajabai Tower atop the library of the Bombay University
which the 'cotton king' donated to the city.

The Decline of Surat

It is easy to understand the success of two of our three
heroes—Jamsetjee Jeejeebhoy and Premchand Roychand.
They rose in tandem with Bombay. Less easier is to
comprehend the achievement of Arjunji Nathji Trawadi, the
Nagar Brahmin, who made his fortune in the turbulent,
warlike conditions of the eighteenth century when the port
city of Surat was in trouble and declining precipitously.

Surat rose during the relatively peaceful and secure times
of the Mughal empire, in the sixteenth and seventeenth
centuries. The Mughals built reasonably good roads and
other infrastructure; they created a stable currency and purer
coinage (although there was the downside of having to
exchange Mughal coins at a loss at the end of each emperor's
reign). As a result, commerce grew, capital accumulated and
merchants flourished. Surat was a jewel in the crown, although
the Mughals in Delhi did not fully realize it, thinking of it

primarily as 'Bandar Mubarak' or Blessed Port, from where the faithful embarked upon their pilgrimage to Mecca.

When the Company arrived in Surat in the early seventeenth century it found that India produced the world's best cotton yarn and textiles, and that too, in enormous quantities. On to this the Company unleashed the dramatic stimulus of European demand, and by 1800 India controlled a quarter of the world's textile trade. 'Indian cottons had transformed the dress of Europe,' David Landes tells us in *The Wealth and Poverty of Nations.* 'Even in cold climes the suitability of cotton for underwear transformed the standards of cleanliness, comfort and health.' As India's market share rose, so did the fortunes of Surat which became a global shipping and financing hub. The trade with the West had to be balanced, however. Since Indians (like the Chinese) did not want anything produced in the West the trade could not be balanced with goods, and so it was balanced with bullion which arrived in massive quantities on the ships of the Company.

At the centre of these transactions were the shroffs and bankers of Surat; and one of the most distinguished among them was Trawadi Arjunji Nathji. A Nagar Brahmin, his family had ancestral connections with Benaras, where they had been trustworthy bankers to the local rajas. With the coming advent of European demand for Benares cottons and silks, the family's attention turned to export of textiles and to their agency at the port of Surat, where Arjunji Nathji glorified the family name, first as a financier of international trade and then as a partner to the Company—as its most Honourable Shroff—in its imperial project.

The shroffs of Surat occupied a proud position in society, as our author informs us, bringing with them a long and hallowed commercial heritage. Although they financed trade throughout the Mughal empire, the spine of their banking activity was the east–west inland trade between Bengal and Surat via Benaras and Awadh. They were respected far and wide and their credit notes and hundis were accepted even in China and Russia. Their word counted and their honour lay in their creditworthiness. As leaders of the Bania Mahajan, a powerful trade body, they were able to influence politics as well. Their clients included the Mughal nobility, business houses across the subcontinent and European trading companies.

However, with the steady erosion of Mughal authority after Aurangzeb's death in 1707, the port city began to feel terribly insecure. Its up-country supply channels were disturbed and its trading networks weakened. The power of the Marathas steadily grew and they began to make persistent demands on Surat's revenues through arbitrary taxes. Faced with an impossible situation the merchants of Surat led by Trawadi had to choose among the declining Mughals, the rising Marathas and the ambitious Company. They chose to align with the Company, not least because its power was backed by a formidable fleet visible in the harbour. Thus the Company gradually infiltrated the governance of the city of Surat via an 'Anglo-Bania alliance'. By 1759 it took over the Castle and the office of the *qiladar*, and thanks to Trawadi influence in Delhi this arrangement was endorsed by the Mughal authority through a *farman*.

Trawadi's decision to ally with the Company was a pragmatic one argues Lakshmi Subramanian. It was informed by 'the conviction that the Company had the wherewithal to make good its debt obligations and that its political and military strength could be relied upon in times of need'. Realistic decisions such as these made it possible for Trawadi to flourish in the conditions of war and a military economy. He got the Company to protect his inter-regional trade, such as the lucrative Surat–Bengal route in silk and cotton; he made a fortune in the war zones by remitting funds to the Company's troops; and when the need arose, he even remitted funds to the Company's headquarters in Bombay and Calcutta via the all-India hundi network. Thus Trawadi became a legend in the backdrop of hostilities during the decline of Surat. Even a waning city offers opportunities to one who has the stomach for risk and the sharpness to back the right horse.

Commerce, Cities, and Governance— An Organic Relationship

The rise of Bombay and the decline of Surat illustrate the organic relationship that binds commerce, cities, and good governance. To ask which comes first is a bit like the conundrum of the chicken and the egg. Ever since it was established in the 1660s, Bombay had tried to woo the powerful merchants of Surat. But it had failed as Surat was flourishing in the peace that prevailed under the Mughals. However, when Mughal authority began to decline and governance weakened in Surat, many merchants and bankers—though not Trawadi —looked to Bombay in the second half of the eighteenth century.

Other towns rose at the same time. The mesmerizing demand for opium and cotton gave birth to new urban centres near the cash-crop fields. Marwari traders in Rajasthan and Gujarati Banias migrated to the cotton- and opium-growing areas of central India in the 1820s to become buyers and financiers of the crops. As a result small towns sprang up in central India, especially in Malwa—today's Madhya Pradesh—in Gujarat, and even in faraway Awadh in the north. In addition to their buying operations the bankers and merchants conducted the business of remittances via hundis on behalf of the big city merchants of Surat and Bombay, while servicing the complex remittance network to meet the needs of troops in the war zones of the Marathas, the English and any other regional power emerging after the Mughals.

With the rise of cities the men of adventure could not be stopped. From across the villages of western India they were quick on their toes to find new means of livelihood offered by the arrival of merchants, wagons and ships. Some hired themselves out as sailors, others joined the merchant marine. Still others joined the caravans of cotton and opium, making their way to the new towns in Malwa and Gujarat, and then onwards to the ports. Artisans and skilled workers followed; first as employees, and then as entrepreneurs. Job opportunities in Bombay's docks and industries attracted increasing numbers. Even though living conditions for the large majority were deplorable, the growth of the cotton and opium trade doubled Bombay's population in the first half of the eighteenth century. The new cities thus offered a new kind of life to the landless masses of the villages to whom it held an irresistible attraction which continues to this day.

Lakshmi Subramanian's three business legends bring to mind other periods of flux and transition when fortunes were made. One of these was medieval Europe when cities were revived in the twelfth century under the stimulus of trade after five centuries of feudal darkness. The incomparable Belgian economic historian, Henri Pirenne describes in his classic *Economic and Social History of Medieval Europe,* the life of a young man named Godric, who, somewhat like our three heroes, made a fortune through his own efforts.

Towards the end of the eleventh century in Lincolnshire, Godric was forced to leave his parents' home and make a living. He became a beachcomber, on the lookout for wreckage thrown up by the waves. 'Shipwrecks were numerous and one fine day he got a windfall, which enabled him to get together a pedlar's pack,' says Pirenne. He amassed a little cash from selling his modest supply of goods. With that he joined a band of merchants whom he met while he was peddling. Soon he had made enough profit which enabled him to form a partnership with another group of merchants who were loading a ship for the purpose of engaging in trade along the coasts of England, Scotland, Flanders and Denmark.

The partnership prospered. Godric used the simple strategy of buying goods which were scarce at the ship's destination and repeated the same thing on the return voyage. Thus he began to export goods to where the demand was greatest and the price, highest. 'In an age when local famines were continual,' says Pirenne, 'one had only to buy a very small quantity of grain cheaply in regions where it was abundant, to realise fabulous profits which could then be increased by the same methods.' In this way Godric made large profits from speculation and this laid the foundation of the first commercial fortunes in medieval Europe. There were many such men who began life with the 'savings of a little pedlar, a sailor, a boatman, or a docker, [which] furnished quite enough capital, if only he knew how to use it'. These first beginnings of commercial capitalism in twelfth-century Europe were accompanied by the creation of new cities in Europe. And why some cities did better than others is partially related to good governance.

Some Lessons from this Book

In writing about the commercial capitalism of eighteen- and nineteenth-century India, Lakshmi Subramanian has brought in a fresh perspective. She has torn down the old, nationalist and Marxist ways of writing business history in which all events were viewed through the lens of colonial and imperial power and through such models as 'dependent' or 'comprador' capitalism. While not denying that it was an age of European domination, she is concerned with how well Indian entrepreneurs adapted to the new opportunities and capitalized on their indigenous ways of doing business.

There are many lessons to be learned from her book. The main one, as I have pointed out, is the organic and self-reinforcing relationship that tied trade, cities, and governance together, and Governor Aungier's advice in 1772 to a new judge which is still one of the best statements on the importance of the 'rule of law'. Another lesson is that free trade holds immense potential for creating the wealth of a nation. Adam Smith and others in eighteenth-century England understood this and hence they fought to break the monopoly of the Company. Once that monopoly was broken, as we saw in Tirthankar Roy's book on the Company in this series, barriers to entry were removed, and this opened up the way for an explosion in private enterprise by Indians and Europeans alike. The enemy of the market and of prosperity is monopoly and lack of competition.

A third lesson is the potential power of private capital to create public good. Sir Bartle Frere showed in Bombay that surplus capital from private speculation in cotton could be diverted to reclaim land from the sea. He believed that private companies would do a better job than the public sector and thus he set the stage for the reclamation of the Backbay. This leads to a fourth and related lesson: in a private–public partnership for the building of infrastructure, there is an ever-present danger of 'crony capitalism' as our author has vividly illustrated in the story of Premchand Roychand and the Bank of Bombay.

A fifth and final lesson is that when trade and free markets make some men hugely wealthy they tend to alleviate the conditions of others as well. There is no evidence in this book that the rise to riches in the three stories recounted here was at the expense of the majority. Trade, in other words, is not a zero-sum game. As we see here the rise of cities accompanies the rise in wealth of the bourgeoisie. This in turn creates its own dynamic. Cities become a magnet of employment opportunities and attract people of all kinds from smaller towns and rural areas. Certainly wealth for a few is not created by impoverishing others.

Gurcharan Das

AUTHOR'S NOTE

WHEN I WAS approached to consider doing a volume on Indian business there was no doubt in my mind about the city I wanted to write about or the period that I wished to look at. Bombay was an obvious choice for more than one reason. It was a city that I knew through its colonial archives when working on my doctoral dissertation almost three decades ago; it was a city whose incomparable business environment was taken for granted in both colonial and postcolonial discourses and where dreams of seeking and finding fortunes were constantly being reiterated in day-to-day conversations and popular film songs. Little wonder then that I chose to look again at the city, at a slice of its nineteenth-century past when local traders and men of commerce confidently consorted in tandem with European associates and held their own amidst challenges and odds in the wake of the articulation of a colonial economy. It was also a period when Bombay began to develop architecturally with causeways being built, land being reclaimed and colossal buildings starting to pepper the urbanscape. The close intersection of capital and land, the connections between business and politics were evident even to the casual visitor when walking along the Fort area. Ambling past stately buildings that once belonged to the Shetias and merchants like Jamsetjee Jeejeebhoy and David Sasoon, the wealth of the city's business elite in the long nineteenth century comes into sharp focus, illustrating how Indian merchants assumed more public and civic responsibilities, imbibing the experience of modernity in quite a material way. Philanthropy, public welfare and liberal political programmes constituted three important facets of merchant self-expression outside the more pressing preoccupations of trade and business. Admittedly such public activities were of little interest to bazaar merchants involved in the more mundane functions of buying and selling, but one may nonetheless legitimately speculate on the potential that the market offered in terms of social interactions. This book explores the mingling of business, consumption, display and public welfare in order to be able to comprehend the complex lives that men of business led in the nineteenth century—a period of opportunity and challenges when money was there to be made and risks were taken. This is, however, primarily a narrative of individual merchants, their personal ambitions and speculative interests that were a part of the city's nineteenth-century history. What I have intended to capture here is a singular dimension within a larger story of early capitalism and its cosmopolitan promise.

The task has not been easy. With the notable exception of the Parsi baron, Sir Jamsetjee Jeejeebhoy who maintained a meticulous and remarkable body of correspondence, the two other protagonists remain somewhat unacknowledged figures. Virtually all that is known of the Surat banker, Trawadi Arjunji Nathji, and the Bombay broker, Premchand Roychand, is from the records of the colonial state. In the case of Trawadi, the 'Honourable Company's shroff' (this is how he is described in documentation of the English East India Company), we have records revealing details of his credit business and his transactions with the Company during the Anglo-Maratha Wars. However, these are essentially business and official records written entirely from the Company's perspective and do not contain any personal details of Trawadi. In the case of Premchand Roychand, the silence is even more telling as we have, for all intents, virtually no references to his dealings except those with regard to some of his charities and a somewhat sharp indictment from the commission that was set up to investigate the causes of the failure of the Old Bank of Bombay in which he featured as a key figure. Piecing together what could be termed as an incoherent narrative was thus both challenging and immensely enjoyable as it gave me an opportunity to discover old Bombay again, visit the Bombay University Library and the state archives to hunt for that elusive detail that makes history-writing so pleasurable.

In writing this study I have profited immensely from fellow academics whose interest in the economic history of India has been a source of both inspiration and support. At a time when economic history has gone out of fashion and there is an overemphasis on all things cultural, it was both refreshing and challenging to attempt a history of Indian trade and business through a biographical axis. Here I wish to record the support that I have received from the staff at the Mumbai State Archives, the Bombay University Library, the National Library and the CSSSC library in Kolkata. A big thanks is also due to my friends, especially Tirthankar Roy and B.R. Tomlinson, who were kind enough to read the typescript and make valuable suggestions, as also my colleagues at the Centre for Studies in Social Sciences whose company and lunchtime *addas* never failed to enthuse me.

Finally I would like to record my sincere appreciation of Gurcharan Das for his encouragement and the copy editors of Penguin India who have been unstinting in their cooperation.

Lakshmi Subramanian
Calcutta, 2012

CHRONOLOGY

1618	Establishment of the English East India Company settlement in Surat
1661	Bombay ceded to the Crown of England as part of a royal dowry to Charles II
1668	Bombay transferred to the Company
1707	Death of Aurangzeb
1750	Building of the Bombay Docks by Lowjee Wadia
1759	The Castle Revolution of Surat; the Company becomes qiladar in Surat
1774	Anglo-Maratha War
1800	Annexation of Surat by the Company
1803–05	Second Anglo-Maratha War
1818	Third Anglo-Maratha War and defeat of the Maratha Confederacy
1822	Establishment of the Elphinstone High School

1839–42   First Opium War

1840   Establishment of the Bank of Bombay

1842   Knighthood bestowed on Jamsetjee Jeejeebhoy

1853   First Indian railway line, from Bombay to
            Thana

1854   Establishment of the Bombay Spinning and
            Weaving Company

1856–60   Second Opium War

1857   Founding of the University of Bombay

PROLOGUE

THIS PROLOGUE IS intended to take readers on a quick tour through the historical landscape of India between 1757 and 1857 when the Mughal empire was superseded—initially by a complex mosaic of regional state systems, and eventually by the English East India Company—the trading body that emerged as the sovereign power of the Indian subcontinent. The process was long and protracted, with significant ramifications for not just the Indian economy and society but also for a larger global economy that was increasingly moving towards what Immanuel Wallerstein called the 'capitalist modern world system'. It was during this epoch that more Indian commodities—raw cotton and opium, among others—became even more global; it was also the time when Indian traders lost some of the advantages they had enjoyed in the markets of Maritime Southeast Asia, and witnessed, even if not silently, the steady extension of the Company's presence in the trading world that they had once dominated. Not all was lost though, as this book will try to demonstrate. More than any other group, merchants were especially astute in piggybacking on the emerging Company-state to seek their fortunes and find new partnerships and new outlets for investment.

A political and historical geography of the subcontinent in this period would have to start with three central coordinates, which in turn would coincide with three distinct temporal regimes. The first is the steady but definitive decline of the Mughal state as a centralized institution that had, for more than two centuries, held the reins of law and order. The Mughal state was replaced by regional state power which assumed very distinct and multiple manifestations, ranging from successor states (where provincial governors who had served the Mughal state took over power) to local social groups who accumulated resources and made a successful bid for political power. These formations occurred over half a century and more, and found concrete expression in the formation of large states such as Hyderabad, Awadh and Bengal as well as others such as the Maratha state in western India and its confederate partners distributed over the subcontinent. In fact the articulation of Maratha power as the second, albeit shadow empire constituted the most important formation for the greater part of the eighteenth and early nineteenth century, providing us with the second coordinate for understanding the politics of transition. Finally, the expansion of Company power and its successful confrontation of the Marathas in 1818 and the formalization of Company rule by the end of the first half of the nineteenth century, when the status of the Company was irrevocably altered by the Charter Act of 1833, constituted the third important coordinate that framed the political transformation of the subcontinent.[1]

Each of these periods or sub-periods overlapped but in all these instances the centrality of the state's function in protecting its subjects and in enabling merchants and markets to operate became a key question. Interestingly the overall perception of contemporaries and later analysts about the century of transition was that conditions moved towards foregrounding the merchant at the centre of operations. The change in the social balance from the mounted knight to the financier and trader was apparent everywhere; while some contemporary chroniclers lamented the ascendancy of the rude and covetous *baqqal*[2] or shopkeeper, others appreciated the influence of mercantilism as an idea that gripped the imagination of regional rulers in the subcontinent.

A short who's who of the major actors in the drama of political change will not be out of place here. We will start with the typical successor states that emerged from within the older provincial set-up of the Mughal empire, namely the states of Bengal, Awadh and Hyderabad, where the former *subahdars* (viceroys) of the Mughal state, frustrated in their efforts to assume greater initiative in the affairs of the central government in Delhi withdrew to their provincial bases where they exercised greater vertical control over the immediate region, and allied with local notables, bankers and landed interests in order to develop more tightly controlled bureaucratic states. All these states were characterized by a vigorous bureaucratic regime that streamlined the system of revenue collection and increased the amount of land revenue collected from peasants and intermediaries. The drive for resources was in part steered by conditions of war and conflict as well as by a new emphasis on filling the older lag between revenue-yielding capacity and state enforcement. With a smaller province to look after and with new social alignments engineered with local elites which included landed intermediaries and merchant bankers and scribes-cum-bureaucrats, a vigorous regional state system came to participate in a new political economy.[3]

The second category of state formation came in the wake of older social movements that translated into political entities when circumstances enabled land-holding groups and peasant cultivators to occupy territory and cohere around an inclusive social philosophy.[4] The best instances of this phenomenon were the Jats, the Sikhs and the Marathas—the Marathas being especially successful in spreading across the subcontinent and becoming an imperial presence—even if it was seen as a poor imitation by Mughal chroniclers. Starting off as a reaction to the dominant hand exerted by the Deccan sultans in revenue extraction, the Marathas represented the maturation of local landed intermediary groups enjoying revenue rights, who used their experience of military service with the Deccan sultans as a vantage point to press for and assume greater status and rights on land.[5] This coincided with the impact that the Bhakti movement had on the consciousness of large sections of society in western India—encouraging peasant cultivators to aspire for a more egalitarian status; the Bhakti movement's transformative potential promised the levelling of caste barriers and also the possibilities of acquiring land in the service of one or the other of the new intermediary chieftains and their families.[6]

Exploiting these conditions of political and social convulsion, Shivaji Bhosle, belonging to an influential Deshmukh family formed an independent polity—the Maratha Swarajya—while braving and resisting the efforts of the Mughal emperor Aurangzeb to contain the rising challenge of Maratha power. Shivaji's death in 1680 was followed by a period of instability and conflict, but by the first quarter of the eighteenth century it became apparent that Maratha power could not be contained or de-recognized. This time it assumed a different dimension—at the core in Poona the reins of power were assumed by the powerful ministerial family of the Peshwas, while a number of Maratha leaders who had been encouraged to head war bands and attack the declining Mughal edifice were assigned spheres of influence which became the nucleus of regional Maratha kingdoms and constitutive components of what came to be known as the Maratha Confederacy. The expansionist politics of the Maratha Confederacy was interrupted by the Afghans under Ahmad Shah Abdali in the fateful Battle of Panipat in 1761 after which Maratha regional states had to confront the political ambitions of the Company.

A similar set of tendencies was evident in the case of both Sikh power in the Punjab as well as of Jat expansion in northern India. The peninsula also saw the emergence of small centralized states that demonstrated a growing interest in maritime trade. The two major states to emerge in this region were the states of Arcot and Mysore which threw up, especially the latter, the most important leaders of resistance against the Company. While the state of Arcot emerged out of the older Mughal province or *suba* as it was known of the

Carnatic, and resembled the successor states of Bengal, Awadh and Hyderabad, the state of Mysore was the creation of a successful soldier of fortune who rose from the ranks to assume de jure authority over the kingdom of Mysore which was nominally under the Wodeyar house. Under Haidar Ali and his successor Tipu Sultan, Mysore rose to the rank of a great power able to hold its own against its neighbours—the states of Arcot, Hyderabad and the Marathas. It resolutely opposed the advance of the Company and was able to give it a stiff fight until the very end.

All these states came under the influence of the Company, referred to by some historians as the 'new power'[7] especially after 1765, when its political intentions assumed more definitive proportions. Starting off as a joint stock-trading company with the blessings of Queen Elizabeth in 1600, it was set up with subscribed capital to garner profit from trading voyages to the East Indies (India and China). It enjoyed a charter from the Crown to exercise monopolistic control over the trade between England and the East Indies. Its domestic operations in India, however, tended to assume a life of its own as servants of the Company in India often developed private trade ventures to supplement their meagre salaries,[8] creating, in the process, a wedge between the head office and the branches.[9] The history of the initial rise of the Company government in India was thus very much a history of its local interests entrenched in the coastal enclaves of Madras, Bombay and Calcutta. These settlements were acquired as part of concessions sought from local authorities. The Company developed these settlements subsequently as bases of its authority and eventually these became the nucleus of the British empire.

What made the Company enclaves so significant? For one, these from the very beginning, enjoyed a distinct identity that was tied up with the Company's preoccupation with making them impregnable against any attack. This involved distinct physical and architectural additions as well as ideological and institutional changes. The cities were fortified with a clear segregation of white and native town-space although this segregation was differently structured in each of these three coastal cities. The cities enjoyed the judicial arrangements put together by the Company for adjudication of claims, and even offered asylum to those seeking protection from their immediate rulers. The Company invited commercial and service groups to take up residence in the new cities and thereby service its own immediate requirements of supply of export items as well as of daily necessities. Additionally the Company tried to develop these centres at the expense of existing port cities with a view to improving the custom duties of the new cities and also to controlling the freight traffic invested in overseas trade by native merchants.[10] The dividends of this policy were not immediately obvious, but there was no doubt that by the middle of the eighteenth century the centre of commercial gravity had clearly shifted to the Company enclaves on the coast. Indian merchants became increasingly predisposed to the new order that these cities represented, moved there to take up residence—even if often on a temporary basis, utilized the Company's judicial mechanisms to resolve disputes related to business and property, and even participated in the municipal politics of the cities.[11]

This book will take up the fortunes of one of these cities— Bombay, where merchant society was in a unique position to carve for itself a special space in the emerging world economy that the Company was part of. In fact the Company through its multilateral trade transactions helped develop Bombay as an early global city. What made Bombay special is a question that will inform the narrative. What was it about Bombay that threw up what Markovits[12] suggests was a more cosmopolitan business environment that enabled local commercial groups to compete more effectively? Do the answers lie merely in the fact that formal colonial rule was delayed in western India? Or does one need to look more closely at the conditions in which relations between the colonial power and the colonized subject came to be constituted? How can one look at urban experiences in a more complex way and detach them from purely economic activities and functions? Can one make the argument that in Bombay the Company found it expedient to negotiate with its local allies who found it to their advantage to project themselves as modest and ideal subjects? Was the situation especially conducive to business in Bombay so much so that the fact of segregation did not create the same psychosis of anxiety that one encounters in Calcutta? I do not have answers to these questions, but I believe these are worth asking, and what I will do therefore is try and identify some of the major elements and moments making up the urban experience in colonial Bombay, and how three individual merchants viewed this colonial transition.

From 1765 the Company from its Calcutta base, armed with a huge revenue surplus from the Diwani—the right to collect revenues from Bengal, Bihar and Orissa sanctioned by the Mughal emperor Shah Alam II—steadily extended its direct control over the subcontinent. This assumed several forms, beginning with the subsidiary alliance by which the Company insisted on states maintaining an English subsidiary force—the upkeep of which was the client state's responsibility. Default in payments meant the state losing control over much of its territory. There were also direct confrontations like in the case of Mysore. The state of Mysore was taken over after the defeat of its rulers, Haidar Ali and Tipu Sultan. With Tipu's final surrender and subsequent death after the Third Mysore War the kingdom was restored to the former ruling house of the Wodeyars, becoming a client princely state. The subjugation of Mysore was followed by the destruction of the Maratha Confederacy in 1818 and thereafter the annexation of the Punjab in 1857 by which time the Company had firmly consolidated its status as the sovereign power of the country. By this time it had also reorganized the revenue and commercial set-up and had provided the basic essentials of an administrative system based on the principles of rule of law. The change was momentous and not without trial and tribulation for Indian society which had to come to grips with a new dispensation. For the Company too the events of the eighteenth century were tantamount to a virtual revolution. The Company as a trading organization was no longer recognizable; it had come a far way from the seventeenth century when its officials—

mostly gauche and bad-mannered—had struggled to make headway in their negotiations with the Mughals. The Company no longer claimed monopoly over anything—the Charter Acts had put paid to that in 1833. However, the Company had through its long career played a key role in connecting India with China and England, and in overseeing a new stage in the development of India's global connections.[13]

1. MERCHANTS AND RULERS IN THE INTERSTICES OF EMPIRE

THE INDIAN MERCHANT has, for a variety of reasons, remained a shadowy subject of history. Notwithstanding the ritual encomiums to the wise and level-headed merchant—often portrayed as a playmate of the young and impetuous prince,[1] or the routine acknowledgement of the cosmopolitan Muslim merchant who dominated the waters of the Indian Ocean in the precolonial era, standard histories have only recently come forward to reclaim the Indian merchant as a subject with agency—who was both pragmatic and cosmopolitan as well as traditional and insular. The conundrum of the 'slippery-merchant' subject who was able and willing to embark on business overseas and at the same time opposed to abandoning tradition has continued to baffle historians and scholars. Was the merchant a modern and liberal subject, the embodiment of individualist enterprise, or was he simply an opportunist who played with capital to merely bolster his traditional attachments? Was he simply a cog in an older wheel of caste and commerce, or was he an active participant in an ever-changing political context? These questions are important and figure increasingly in the more recent studies on trade and business in precolonial and colonial India. This is a significant departure from conventional scholarship on Indian business that has tended to frame its inquiries within the paradigms of development and underdevelopment.[2]

By and large even when there has been a concerted attempt at viewing merchant enterprise in India—both in the context of precolonial as also the colonial/modern period—the investigation has inevitably became enmeshed in narratives of capitalist development: why this development did not happen in India at the same time that it did in the north European world; whether the Indian environment was intrinsically hostile to business enterprise; or whether it was colonial intervention that checkmated its complete potential. Hence there has been a general tendency to confront merchant subjects with a volley of questions that are not always sensitive to context. Some of these questions relate to economic rationality and social behaviour. For instance were the merchants bearers of capitalism, agents with rational business practices or parasites sucking the blood of toiling peasants? Were they slavish subjects of imperial authority or were they in fact devious hedgers who always sat on the fence waiting for an opportunity to make a quick buck? Some answers have been forthcoming. There are several seminal accounts of merchants in precolonial India, of merchant circulation in the Indian Ocean, as also of their resilience in adapting to change. There are also remarkably imaginative readings of texts occasionally authored by merchants—such as the *Ardhakathanak* of the seventeenth-century Jain trader Banarsidas—which stress the capabilities of merchants to negotiate multiple levels of authority and even inhabit multiple selves.[3] However, in popular imagination merchants have remained cardboard cut-outs—archetypal figures hunched over their accounts, deviously buying land from indigent peasantry and remaining huge landowners even if they went overseas—in short, *dukkawallas* (store-keepers) alienated from the larger environment. As a result there is little that exudes a positive impression of merchant enterprise. Further there is a complete absence of excitement in unearthing the drama of business enterprise, of its twists and turns and highs and lows, except as discrete episodes in a complicated trajectory of India's development during the colonial era. This is surprising considering that elementary sense suggests that the activity of planning and embarking on a venture and taking decisions in the face of uncertainty and perhaps even hostility should make for interesting reading.

The facts at hand or even the interpretations of them do not merit a bland portrayal—for some of the more recent scholarship that has recast the history of India of the eighteenth and nineteenth centuries foregrounds the initiative of the gentry, the scribe, the merchant and the banker in participating aggressively in a changing environment, and in the process embracing a complex orientation to the world in which they operated. We can in fact venture to tell a story of individuals who took risks, who made spectacular gains and suffered enormous losses, and in the process engaged with many of the tangible and intangible facets of the functioning environment. Thus one can make a case for a new kind of business and economic history.[4] This history would focus not so much on problems of interpretation but on life histories and narratives that suggest a range of complex impulses informing merchant behaviour at particular epochs in India's history—in this case the period between the mid-eighteenth and the mid-nineteenth century as well as the period thereafter which constituted the high noon of imperialism. During the first period—the century of transition—Mughal sovereignty was replaced by the political hegemony of the English East India Company—a body of merchants who won an empire for their masters in Britain. In the century that followed, imperial rule subordinated India to the status of a key colony whose centrality was acknowledged by one and all.

What was so remarkable about the century of transition? One could answer this question from multiple vantage points and each would be as legitimate as the other. From the point of view of politics and political claimants, the most noticeable change was the displacement of Mughal authority and regional state power by the Company which slowly nibbled away at the decaying edifice of Mughal rule, and by a cunning combination of stratagems, diplomacy and warfare, became the ultimate master of the subcontinent. What underpinned this story was conflict—indeed an endemic state of conflict constituted the overall environment in which states and their subjects, rulers and merchants functioned, struggling to keep ventures afloat, regimes intact and revenues secure.

Intermittent wars, the gradual erosion of an older political and moral economy, the breakdown of law and order in the wake of war and political conflict were part of this story of transition—a transition to which eighteenth-century Urdu poets in north India gave their voice in eloquent laments on the declining city of Delhi.[5] For these poets, whose world view corresponded to that of the Mughal aristocracy, the century of transition was a veritable apocalypse when the world was turned upside down—upstarts became kings, and as a popular saying went, beggars paid obeisance to whoever wore the crown—in short, ties of loyalty had fallen apart and anyone with power attracted a following.[6] In this milieu merchants were especially despised—as creditors with claims on assignments and known to drive hard bargains, and as power brokers and kingmakers—they were scorned upon as they moved into positions of importance created by changing circumstances.

Thus for merchants the century of transition was not only one of risk and uncertainty but also equally of opportunity, where everything depended on how effectively they responded to the challenges of political transition. Some of them, like our protagonists, did this with alacrity—responding to both the changing political economy of transition as well as to the advent of the Company as a new political aspirant. The new political economy was constituted in part by the changed revenue arrangements that involved working with anticipated incomes guaranteed by bankers' sureties as well as by the increasing requirements on the part of regional states for swift and easy credit transfers occasioned by the political and military arrangements of the period. Thus in less than half a century, merchants—the Jagat Seths in Bengal, the Bania bankers and firms like the house of Trawadi Shree Krishna Arjunji Nathji (hereafter referred to as Trawadi Arjunji Nathji) and Jagannathdas Laldas Parekh in Surat, traders—the Hari Bhaktis in the Maratha Confederate areas, the Benaras bankers of the house of Gopaldas Manohardas, and the house of Lala Kashmiri Mal in Awadh—each of whom were central to the smooth functioning of power regimes and subsequently to the political project of the Company—became the real power brokers.[7]

Did the emerging alignment of finance and power foster and ensure the steady maturation of merchant fortunes? Did it enable the accumulation of capital, providing it with a context that would witness the leap into enterprise and entrepreneurship? Or was the expectation quickly belied by new challenges and constraints that came forth in the aftermath of the Company's hegemony—forcing the merchants once more to think on their feet and scrabble around for strategies that defied conventional formulae? The trajectory and telos of business enterprise in western India were largely contingent on the political context that made available a particular set of options which the merchant society responded to with caution and intelligence. It is a story that deserves telling if only to contest the usual assumptions about the lack of mobility in Indian society or to contest the apparent lack of rationality and agency in business practice. This is not to suggest that business success was immediately translated into archetypal aspirations of bourgeois modernity of the western variety. In fact there was a complex set of negotiations with the emerging and changing environment even as there was an instinctual invocation of residual traditions of practice.[8] Just how these were played out will be clear on an examination of the lives of our individual protagonists.

Any standard history of business enterprise and entrepreneurship takes, as its starting point, a close examination of the environment or milieu—geographical and structural—within which the lives of individuals and collectivities were played out.[9] This is not to downplay the importance of a political event like colonialism both in its early incarnation as well as in its subsequent manifestation, but to simply locate the nature and dynamism of enterprise in a larger social and physical environment. The specific geographic region which I shall focus on is western India which also happened to be nineteenth-century India's premier maritime region where business and capital accumulation assumed a critical mass. Blessed with a littoral that supported a range of medium- and large-sized ports and a productive hinterland that had attained a high level of skill and efficiency in textile manufacture, the region was home to a vibrant merchant population that from very early times played a key role in trade and exchange.[10]

Prominent among the merchant communities were Hindu and Jain groups from Gujarat and Rajasthan who dominated the business of brokerage and banking, and built up impressive reserves of capital as well as close working relationships with the state authorities. These groups were identified broadly as

'Banias'—a term that is not easy to explain with precision.[11] It was seen historically as a category that blends caste and occupation, accommodating eighty-four (a conventional figure endorsed by some external observers as well) Jain and Vaishnav clans or *kulas*—Oswal, Agarwal, Kapol, Porwal, Shrimali, Medatval and others formed this group that simultaneously accommodated other high-caste Hindu groups traditionally associated with trade and commerce. The eighteenth-century author of the *Mirat-i-Ahmadi* identified eighty-four divisions within the community of Meshris (Hindus) and Shravaks (Jains), and observed that they were collectively referred to as baqqals or shopkeepers.[12] The author Ali Muhammad Khan also alluded to the extensive distribution of Shravaks virtually everywhere in Hindustan. The association of certain kinds of trading activity and retail with the Banias was important as it made them more than just members of a caste category. This is evident from both indigenous historical accounts as well as from later European observations that emphasized two important features: the caste structure and ethics; and the identification of economic and mercantile functions with the community—collectively understood, if not designated, as Bania. For instance the British Resident at Baroda, Colonel Alexander Walker, mentions quite categorically in his report on the trades and castes of western India that the 'Wanee deals in every specie of merchandise, but particularly in grain. He trafficks also largely in cloths and professes brokerage and practices usury in every shape.'[13]

Colonel Walker also referred to the fact that several

Brahmins, especially Nagar Brahmins in Gujarat, practised these professions. As he observed, shroffs were 'generally Banians in Guzerat', but added that they were frequently 'of the caste of Bramans'—some of the latter being 'the most opulent individuals in the world.'[14] Equally important was the fact that their interests were safeguarded by a body known as the Bania Mahajan that represented the business interests of the community as a whole. In Gujarat this body was seen as a council of sorts representing a group of people engaged in the same occupation, with an elected, and often hereditary, headman. Sometimes it also indicated a body governing all the Bania merchants in a town but it also applied generally to any assembled or collective body of merchants regardless of *jati* or creed.[15]

The influence that the community wielded was clearly linked to its commercial acumen and its ability to provide services especially in terms of financial and credit support to a whole range of clients. The community prided itself on securing the assistance of robust community networks and maintaining a cohesive identity structured around personal practices of faith and diet. This was evident to most observers and commentators who were struck by the Banias' strict adherence to vegetarianism and the respect they showed for all forms of life. The *Mirat-i-Ahmadi* recalls an interesting story of origins and the social history of commercial networks:

> In bygone days, a Shevra came to a village in Marwar. As there was no Shravak in the village, the poor wanderer could not beg his bread and starved through the night. At midnight, the village chief's son was bitten by a

snake and was dying. The Shevra knew [how] to cure
him and sent word to the chief that he would cure him
if he became a follower of the Shevras. His aim was to
have some Shravaks in the village who could look after
the needs of the wandering Shevras. The chief accepted
the condition. The Shevra cured his son and in this
way, the chief and Rajputs of the village became
Shravaks.[16]

The advantages of such networks were especially valuable to
traders in their quest not only to mobilize capital and
credibility, but also to access information that was so crucial
to the success of business ventures. The willingness to travel
and set up business firms was then predicated on working
through a caste and business network, alongside a disposition
to risk-taking which was intrinsic to business ventures; all
this was partly informed by the environment in western
India that spawned and supported these mobile merchant
communities. Scholars have suggested that the fragile agrarian
base in the more arid areas of western and north-western
India threw up opportunities for commercial investment and
created what is known as the 'push factor to emigration'.[17]
Added to this was the depth of manufacture in regions such
as Gujarat, Kathiawar and Kutch, where cotton production
and textile manufacture ensured the availability of a huge
export staple—one which was fostered by conditions of
political stability especially under the Mughals.

The seventeenth century in fact saw the pre-eminence of
Gujarat as the most developed maritime region of Mughal
India and the emergence of Surat as its blessed port (Bandar

Mubarak)[18] that served as the embarkation point for Haj. Given the extensive trade that Surat commanded with the ports in western-Indian Ocean and with other feeder regions and ports in the Indian Ocean—both coastal and overseas entrepôts—it was but inevitable that the region's mercantile communities would enjoy their share of the boom. The influence they commanded over the business of brokerage was partly due to their financial base and the fact that they were in a position to fund the chain of supply from the manufacturer to the exporting merchant. Of course the contractors who were in direct touch with the manufacturers were drawn from a miscellany of groups—identified in the Company records as Bania, Bora and Parsi; their services were crucial in linking up the transactions between the exporting merchant and the primary manufacturer. It was they who formed the channel to organize the labour of the workmen and provide the necessary support to the workers in times of need.[19]

The penetration of merchant-capital into the production process was significant in precolonial India, and while it did not replicate the conditions that helped production to take off in western Europe, the linkages between capital and both production and supply, were crucial in providing commercial experience and apprenticeship for subsequent enterprise. At the same time the expansion of foreign and inland trade brought a substantial inflow of bullion that had to be converted into the regnal coin which was necessary for both revenue payments and commercial investment. The emphasis on the regnal coin as the only admissible instrument of transaction was derived from the Mughal state's insistence that only the coins of the ruler in power—usually freshly minted at the time of accession—were to be regarded as legal tender. This meant that on every occasion of accession, old coins were exchanged for new ones at lower rates, and as a consequence of wear and tear led to the diminution of the silver content of the *sicca* rupee. It also meant that all foreign coins had to be exchanged for local regnal ones.[20]

The business of money-assaying and money-changing was thus crucial to the working of the imperial financial system and it was here that the Bania banking community intervened to become a vital element in its working. Technically there was a Mughal mint where bullion and foreign coins were minted; but in practice the overload that the mint suffered from forced merchants and exporters to approach private bankers who were allowed to perform the functions of assaying and changing. Also the actual running of the mint was in the hands of the *sarraf*s, or bankers, who farmed out the minting rights. The sarrafs of the mint charged the importer for the minting time which could be as long as six months. As bullion imports into Surat from the Red Sea generally came during the months of August and September, there was a huge rush to get this converted, which was when the sarrafs drove a hard bargain.[21] While one could argue, as some historians have, that it was the expanding European trade that enabled Bania brokers and bankers to assume such influence, it must be kept in mind that Asian trade continued to be the most important segment for India's overseas trading economy and that the enhanced security provided by the

Mughal state was an enabling factor in the expansion and consolidation of inland trade and financial networks.

The facilitating financial instrument in securing and anchoring the inland and export trading economy was the hundi, an old mechanism resembling a bill of exchange. The hundi was the most characteristic credit institution in India, promising payment usually after a specified period at a particular place and allowing a discount that included insurance charges and other service costs. In long-distance trade this became the standard form of payment that not only met the requirements for ever-expanding credit, but also minimized the risks involved in transmission of cash. Simply put the hundi was a written order, usually conditional, made by one person to another for the payment of a specified sum of money on demand or after a specified period of time, subject to discount, at a specified place. What this made possible was the transfer of funds for easy and safe remittances and also, over time, its extended use as a credit instrument. In this case the holder of the hundi, rather than waiting to present it before the drawer's agent, used the hundi to take a loan by transferring it through endorsement to the lender. Hundi operations were almost entirely monopolized by Bania sarrafs who operated a vibrant hundi market that serviced business at multiple levels. Banias as village shopkeepers and commission agents or *arhatiyas*—like shroffs and bankers—controlled the levers of business and spread their *kothi*s (branch office) and agencies on a pan-Indian scale. It was the extension of the economic and credit frontier that gave the community members a huge fillip to expand their influence, and in the long run to emerge as influential capitalists even if their profiles did not match up to any strict European prototype. It was this community of bankers and brokers that threw up our protagonists—the Brahmin banker Trawadi Arjunji Nathji, the maverick 'cotton king' Premchand Roychand and finally, the Parsi magnate Jamsetjee Jeejeebhoy whose participation in the remittance business assumed global ramifications.

A prehistory of capital in western India inevitably begins with the commercial advances of Mughal India. The sixteenth and seventeenth centuries saw the flowering of India's export and inland trade, enabling merchant-capital accumulation that was deployed in several sectors which were seen as viable and profitable. The financing and marketing of the textile trade constituted a major segment of indigenous business, as did remittance through hundis. Remittance was a key activity but one that, in the seventeenth century, remained largely oriented towards commercial transactions and not political projects as was the case during the following century of transition. A huge turnover in terms of textile exports and bullion imports was supported by a robust system of inland trade and credit transfers as well as by an efficient infrastructure guaranteed by the Mughal state. Merchants of all hues could count on the formal structure of governance even if there were instances of individual caprice.[22] By and large the merchants preferred to toe the line of the ruling administration and did not see this as compromising autonomous action—a value that underpinned merchant ethos. From all accounts the community saw *vyapar*, or business, as a calling; as a preference over service because it seemed to promise greater independence of action and decision-making.

This aptitude for an independent calling was augmented by certain social values and practices as well as by ideology. Especially among Jains the articulation of religion as a personal quest rather than as a hierarchical organization produced a very different relationship to both business and spending on charity—in other words the accumulation of wealth for subsequent use and investment and thereby to gain merit was an important guiding principle. Thus merit-seeking became a powerful incentive to action.[23] At the same time there are references to the way Jain laymen were taught business practices in the *Upashraya* (likened often to the Quaker meeting house). Along with such training and apprenticeship there was a strong sense of guild loyalty promoted by membership in the Bania Mahajan, which was not a caste organization. To belong to the Mahajan went hand in hand with a certain image of themselves as traders with honour—the idea of *abru* that Douglas Haynes talks about in connection with the self-image of Bania merchants.[24]

Creditworthiness was seen as crucial in sustaining the reputation of one's own family-firm as well as in providing the necessary scaffolding for the larger business structure in which one operated. This meant two things at a practical and pragmatic level: one, as mentioned before, ensuring a degree of support from the government by adopting a positive stance; and two, establishing and maintaining informal mechanisms of trust. Both of these were in fact seen as absolutely central to the working of business in the early modern period especially when there were no formal laws of contract in place. The importance of informal trust and honour came into dramatic effect, for example, on the occasion of the riots in Surat in August 1795, when the Bania Mahajan in Surat petitioned the Company to take immediate steps to improve law and order and safeguard the community's person and property which had been attacked by Muslim rioters. It is worthwhile quoting from this petition just to understand the ways in which the community members saw their reputation and their business in late eighteenth-century Surat and the meaning they attached to their political connection with the Company:

> The entire belief that property is perfectly secure in the house of a shroff forms what is called his credit, which more than actual money is the instrument of his dealing and the great source of his profits—those who come to trade in the city either bring bills on the shroffs or lodge the produce of their goods with them during their stay . . . Large sums are deposited with the shroffs at Surat . . . also the little savings of those who do not trade are lodged with shroffs, portions of widows in the Bania caste. For all these sums deposited, no receipts are given, the books of the shroffs and the opinion of their faith and substance are the total dependence of the people who deal with them; from this it is clear how much credit depends on the belief of their effectual protection by the government they live under. We are concerned that the plunderers of Adit Ram Shroff destroyed the accounts of his shop on which the

ascertainment of property of others wholly depends
from whence it may be inferred that on alarm of this
tumult and knowledge of this circumstance, there may
be a general demand on all shroffs for foreign accounts
and that their credit in this place will not be amply
restored until they are visibly under the protection of
the English government.[25]

Two things are obvious from this petition: one, the existence
of a strong sense of solidarity among the aggrieved merchant
community of Surat; and two, their clearly articulated
preference for the support of the Company in order to
safeguard their position in the city against a decaying
administration that had allowed a riot situation to occur and
escalate. To understand both these tendencies and their
provenance one must look at the immediate temporal context
of the eighteenth century in which the Hindu/Jain Bania
merchant community of Surat, indeed, of the entire region
of western India, operated, so as to be able to understand the
implications of the political transition for indigenous business.
There were several distinct phases in the process of
transition—each stage throwing up a different set of options
for those far-sighted enough to take up the opportunity.

The first phase of transition was associated with the decline
and erosion of Mughal power and authority in Surat—
Gujarat's premier port city, and in Ahmedabad—the
provincial capital, and with the gradual assertion of the
Company's power along the west coast, with its locus in
Bombay. What these developments meant on the ground
was quite simple and amounted to: first, a gradual erosion of

the Mughal administrative structure; and second, the assertion of political and fiscal demands by other claimants, notably the Marathas, followed at a later date by the Company. This was of course not immediately apparent. Thus in 1700 the situation would have shown no untoward signs of instability to a casual observer. Bankers and traders went about their business as usual even if there were the small tremors of uncertainty that they were accustomed to especially during moments of succession and change at the centre.[26]

In 1700 power in western India was largely invested with the Mughal administration in Gujarat, with pockets of autonomy exercised by coastal powers of Maratha extraction along the Konkan—the Angrias of Kolaba and the Desais of Savantwadi—as well as the Portuguese in Daman and the Company in Bombay. The locus of Mughal authority lay in south Gujarat, while farther north along the coasts of Kutch and Kathiawar, political control was far more fragmented with a more flexible set of arrangements overseen by smaller Rajput and Kathi chiefs who exercised their authority in the region. Most of the chiefs in Kathiawar paid tribute to the Mughal state, while in south Gujarat the Mughal administration remained intact, giving little cause for concern to merchants or peasants. Trade seemed to operate under conditions of relative prosperity—the presence of the Surat commercial fleet in the waters of the Arabian Sea indicated quite clearly where the balance of power lay and merchants carried on with their business.[27]

Beneath the apparent calm, however, ripples of uncertainty were forming. The death of the Alamgir (Aurangzeb) in

Delhi, the succeeding decades of factional politicking and the disruption of communication networks by the dissenting Marathas had tangible consequences even for far-flung regions like Gujarat. At an immediate level the failure of the provincial administration to contain the disaffection and ambitions of its own officers and to resist the growing demands of the Marathas—the principal rival of the Mughals—was apparent, while at a more long-term level the disruption of communication networks undercut the supply channels for the Gujarati merchants.

The subsequent decades saw the Marathas assume greater control over Ahmedabad and Surat. This took the form of actual physical control over some territories as well as a demand on the city's revenues. The Maratha occupation of the *athavisi*, or twenty-eight villages, surrounding Surat, from which the city administration drew its revenues, put extreme pressure on the ruling group which then resorted to the desperate measure of taxing the merchants to stave off the crisis. This decision had disastrous implications for the city merchants especially as they were operating amidst severe constraints produced by conditions of political insecurity which interrupted supplies, and by the escalating competition from the English and European private merchants in the Indian Ocean whose activities were creating a glut in overseas markets. These European and English private traders made full use of their special relationship with the Company to gain leverage, and between their access to ships of larger tonnage and their superior naval strength that could deal with piracy in the high seas, they were able to undercut the

Surat merchants in the volatile West Asian markets—these markets were already reeling under the effects of the decline of the Ottoman and Safavid empires in Turkey and Persia respectively. Thus for the Surat merchants the crisis of the eighteenth century was a very real one and by the 1750s the old system of traffic was in tatters. Politically, merchants were confronting the exactions of a desperate ruling class that had ceased to govern, as well as the aspirations and aggrandizement of private merchants and the Company— that began to entertain political ambitions as a means of strengthening and expanding its commercial operations.[28]

The emergence of the Company as a political aspirant in western India was tied closely to its commercial interests. From its headquarters in Bombay and its trading station in Surat the Company focused initially on developing its island city as an alternative to Surat—persuading merchants and service groups to migrate by offering conditions of better security and benefits. Subsequently Company authorities developed a more explicit political agenda by making a bid for coastal control through their naval force, the Bombay Marine, which enforced the hegemony of the English trading pass—superseding those of other coastal powers. Simultaneously they began to infiltrate into the local administration of Surat by taking up the claims of their client-merchants (i.e., those who worked for them as brokers and credit suppliers), contesting the demands and jurisdiction of the ruling administration of the city, and then in 1759, actually taking control of the Castle (the *qila* in Surat) and the office of the qiladar. Behind the coup or the 'Castle

Revolution' as it came to be known, lay the support of a sizeable section of the city's Bania merchants—led principally by Jagannathdas Laldas and endorsed by Trawadi Arjunji Nathji—who had decided to side with the Company in the newly emerging political dispensation.[29]

It is however, important to neither exaggerate the power of the Company in Surat at this time nor to overstate the cohesiveness of the Anglo-Bania order. The fact was that apart from the Anglo-Bania order, Surat, during the transition, was the site of multiple power blocs organized around the Marathas, the existing Mughal administration as well as European trading companies like those of the French and the Dutch, with merchants of all denominations and ethnicities coming together around one bloc or another. The English bloc would appear to have slowly gained an edge over its rivals, with the result that the Anglo-Bania order held fast and eventually enabled the Company to achieve paramountcy in the entire region.[30]

It was crucial for the Banias to ensure a degree of stability in governance so that trade and production structures could be maintained, albeit at a lower level, and also to identify new possibilities for business in changing times. For the other merchants—notably Muslim shippers and exporters whose trade and freight business were directly undermined both by the Company's operations as well as those of the private traders who managed to enforce a virtual monopoly over Surat's trade and shipping in the western-Indian Ocean—the Company's expanding presence was a threat, and one that they could hardly counter with efficacy. For the Parsis who were making their way up the echelons of trade and business from a manufacturing background, the alliance with the European trading companies and the latter's rising demand for textiles was a positive development. The Parsis were also among the first to respond to the call for settling in Bombay, where they quickly forged important connections and built up their businesses, ranging from dockyard building to victualling services.[31]

From the early eighteenth century, Bombay the island city of the Company began to attract migrants from other parts of western India—notably Surat—as they recognized how the balance of power was slowly shifting in favour of the Company and thus responded to the obvious benefits that the Company connection seemed to promise. Admittedly Bombay was still, in terms of its commercial and business profile, a poor second to Surat, and it remained thus for the greater part of the eighteenth century—a complementary or satellite city of the latter. Most of the Surat merchants maintained branch offices in Bombay and while they were able to carve out a space for themselves in the new city's business districts, their ventures and capital were firmly rooted in the older and traditional centres of Surat and Ahmedabad. What was significant, however, was their conscious decision to align with the Company against the ruling class as well as its chief adversary, the Marathas, and promote the Company's expansionist politics, which in the course of time became the principal determinant of their enterprise.

The Marathas in fact held the key to the politics of the larger region. While their presence was peripheral in Surat and did not make a dent in the coastal hegemony of Bombay, the same could not be said of, for example, the region of Kathiawar, where the situation was quite different as far as political configurations went. By the mid-1730s the Marathas under the leadership of the Gaekwads were able to exercise control over the semi-independent chiefs of the province through what was known as the '*mulkgiri* expeditions', and in 1753 occupied the provincial capital of Ahmedabad. This event marked the definitive transfer from Mughal to Maratha power. As the century wore on the mulkgiri expeditions became increasingly oppressive forcing political aspirants to contemplate alliances with the Company, which however, waited right until the turn of the nineteenth century to consider a change in policy as far as Kathiawar was concerned.[32] In Kutch further north, the relative isolation of the province saved it from the Mughal–Maratha clashes for some time, but while it was spared the Maratha mulkgiri it faced from the latter half of the eighteenth century, both the onslaught of Sind's expansion from the north and the politics of maritime predation adopted by most of the smaller claimants along the coast.

The second phase in the politics of transition, which may loosely be identified with the aftermath of the Castle Revolution of 1759, was characterized principally by conditions of conflict—localized at some times, more generalized at other times. The event as seen before had brought the Company in as a formal component in the power structure. It exercised this right somewhat tentatively in the beginning, primarily to bolster its trade interests and those of its servants, and deflect any possible encroachments by the Marathas who were definitely its most serious rivals. South of Surat and Bombay, the Company's Bombay Marine maintained a close vigil over any coastal political aspirant, and with the defeat and final subjugation of minor coastal princely families like the Angrias and the Desais, the hegemony of the Company's pass was no longer in doubt.

Beyond the Western Ghats the Maratha leadership under the Peshwas reigned supreme from their base in Poona, while the senior chiefs of the Maratha Confederacy (Sindhia, Bhonsle and Gaekwad) extended their control over central India, Gujarat and Kathiawar. The Company, strapped for cash and with only a fragile foothold in Bombay, did not dare to confront the Marathas. It was only after the 1780s that it made feeble attempts to secure a foothold in the cotton-rich tracts of south Gujarat, like Broach. In 1772 Broach was occupied on the pretext of the Nawab's embezzlement of revenue payments, and retained for ten years, until in 1782, by the Treaty of Salbai, the city once more changed hands and went over to Mahadji Sindhia.

The late 1770s were thus a period of political insecurity and tension—Maratha pressure in Kathiawar, the Mughal–Maratha stand-off in Gujarat and the First Anglo-Maratha War. This was followed in the closing years of the century by more intense conflicts that coincided with the imperialist project of Lord Wellesley. Also outside the western littoral the second half of the eighteenth century saw a steady penetration of the Company's force and a series of skirmishes as well as serious wars—the Mysore Wars, the Third Battle of Panipat—and the escalation of tensions between indigenous powers. This ensured what may be called a pandemic of conflict, forcing merchants, among other groups, to function amidst changing, if not trying, circumstances.[33]

What did these political developments signify for merchants and traders? Admittedly war was not always seen as a disaster. After all the ability of political claimants to wage war was predicated on their ability to raise money by some means or the other whenever the military situation demanded it and in quantities that were substantial. During times of war the existing fiscal structure could not always be sufficient, and it became paramount to find and tap adequate resources and help to maintain and even salvage trade flows so that bullion supplies remained uninterrupted. At the same time military operations generated a huge demand for the remittance of funds across great distances so as to keep the military satisfied and ensure the provisioning of troops. This became even more critical when armies required local currency to look after their needs—something that only bankers with extensive connections could ensure. Thus under the circumstances no state could afford to antagonize the merchants or attack the credit structure, however, rickety it may have been at any given point of time. The century of transition in India was no different—it was in this context that merchant groups like the Banias played a singularly significant role as they came forward to undertake financing and remittances for administrative, commercial and military operations.[34]

The ramified dimensions of the Bania enterprise came into full display after 1750, when the Company, the Marathas and the Mughals (or what little remained of their local and provincial strength) made a bid to enlist the support of the merchants and shroffs to tide them over, both immediately and for the long term. For the shroffs what ultimately mattered was how reliable the debtor was and how a smooth level of trade and traffic could be secured by good governance. Good faith was essential on the part of both parties—an old precondition that kings had often been customarily forced to acknowledge. For instance in the 1430s the king of Aragon exhorted his treasurer to pay attention to good faith so that merchants never had reason to doubt his word. As he communicated to his treasurer in Barcelona:

> You will do us great service if you ensure that the merchants in these parts have full confidence in us by means of letters sent to them from other merchants there to whom you have given security; so that should the need arise for us to take other bills, we should not be obliged to go looking for guarantors or pledges and they will have no reason to doubt our word and our bills of exchange. Besides shaming and disparaging us, this causes us loss because their lack of confidence in our credit makes the bills more expensive than usual.[35]

These observations were equally applicable to the situation in late eighteenth-century India whose political economy was almost entirely determined by war and war-related demand, and was critically dependent on the availability of commercial and reliable credit arrangements extended by loyal bankers. The configuration of the commercial and credit network in late Mughal India was largely determined by new state formations and the reorientation of inland trade routes.[36] The credit flows were held in place by a new degree of regional and inter-regional trade connections that coalesced in the aftermath of regional state-building. As mentioned earlier the death of Aurangzeb and the decay of Mughal state institutions was quickly followed not just by a regrouping of regional satraps, but by the enormous concentration of financial power in the hands of premier banking houses like that of the Jagat Seths and thereafter of the Benaras-based Gopaldas Manohardas and of Lala Kashmiri Mal in Awadh.

Between 1757 (Battle of Plassey), when the Company—thanks largely to the assistance of the banking house of the Jagat Seths and other local power brokers—assumed real authority over the Bengal administration, and 1781 (Treaty of Salbai), when the Marathas and the Company settled for a temporary truce, merchants and bankers emerged as a major entity working a complex trading and political economy—and deploying a range of strategies and practices to earn profit and find ways of investing their accumulated capital. Thus two broad features characterized the eighteenth-century transition economy: the first was the acceleration of commercialization and cash flows resulting from a wider application of revenue farming, and the alignment of the revenue-extracting mechanisms with local credit and banking groups; and the second was the reorientation of trade routes and their alignment with newly emerging configurations of tribute transfers undertaken by regional states. What this meant on the ground was that new levels and routes of trade began to criss-cross the subcontinent; this was also a consequence of the emergence of regional states such as Bengal, Awadh, Hyderabad, Benaras, Mysore and the Maratha Confederacy, and on these were overlaid the credit and remittance network operated by local- and regional-level bankers whose monetary operations serviced commercial and political transactions.[37]

Bankers benefited from this regional redistribution of power and trade and followed the trails of war and conquest as well as of trade and pilgrimage, which as in the case of the Maratha Confederacy and Punjab, became a state-sponsored project as well. Rulers found it to their advantage to oversee fairs and pilgrimage-related activities—a concrete illustration of which was the spectacular rise of Benaras as the great banking city of the eighteenth century. Bernard Cohn's masterly study of the political system in Benaras made the important point that the main officials of the Benaras Raj[38] were tax farmers who began as bankers of the same caste as of the ruling house and took service with the reigning raja as a means of making a quick buck. The emergence of the house of Gopaldas Manohardas testified to this development just as the pre-eminence of Trawadi Arjunji Nathji in Surat and his alignment with the Company as its 'honourable shroff' illustrated how the expansion of the new power, i.e., the Company, was closely implicated in the dynamics of indigenous credit.

One must pause here to reflect on the opportunities and challenges the merchants would have had to respond to in the century of transition. Once the initial shock of dislocation had faded and the decay of older arterial routes and the scaling down of business ventures had been factored in, merchants everywhere were left with the choice to align themselves with the immediate local power centre. The consolidation of regional states gave a fillip to trade and manufacturing activity, and the result, as mentioned earlier, was a renewed impetus to cross-country routes. This was possible because evidently bankers and merchants continued to find channels of investment, and because their importance in the revenue administration gave them a particular edge. Transition made viable close connections between capital and state power, and rendered the merchants key political actors. Thus the revenue collector and the *sahukar* worked in tandem in the countryside, while the banker in the city could count on the support of the municipal administration especially as his bills mediated inter-treasury transfers. English officials and administrators did not always take a favourable view of the matter even if they used the local credit connection themselves with alacrity and regularity. Take the case of Sir John Malcolm who in his Malwa memoir refers to the close nexus between power and profit, even if he was loath to refer to traders as capitalists. In fact his indictment was damning:

> There are few, if any, of the bankers and merchants that can be termed capitalists, and they have been so mixed and soiled in late revolutions, that those who have not been wholly ruined in fortune, have lost much of that character and those correct habits which belong to this class of men in other parts of India.[39]

Malcolm's reservations notwithstanding the bankers who were both casualties and beneficiaries of transition were shrewd and astute players. Relying on their familial connections they had their ears close to the ground and were alert to any changes in the political register. By the mid-1770s they were more than aware of the importance of the Company's power and its ramifications. As the Diwan of Bengal, Bihar and Orissa, and as the dominant partner in a series of relationships with local country powers, the Company was recognized as the most important power-holder and more importantly, the most reliable in terms of loan repayment to bankers and creditors. This was evident when bankers intervened to respond to the Company's call for remittance services to its various stations and settlements, to fight wars against those who continued to resist the Company. The result was a slow and incremental partnership cohering around the Company's axes of power—the bankers moving in with their funds and credit in order to bankroll the imperial project of annexation.

Two factors made this possible: one was the consideration that the Company had the financial power to make good the loans secured; and the other was the existence of a trade network that made money movements possible, closely aligned with the movement of goods. Bankers did not lend or remit money out of the goodness of their heart—this was a well-thought-out and pragmatic response to a situation where the possibilities of commercial prospects were, ironically enough, provided by conditions of war and a military economy on the one hand, and by regional and inter-regional groupings of trade on the other. Thus the Surat–Bengal trade in silk and cotton provided the skeletal framework with which the bankers operated to remit huge sums of money for the benefit of the Company establishments in Bombay and Fort William. Bankers in other regional groupings like the Punjab and eastern Awadh worked to seal the all-India hundi network even as the influence of the Company's trading poles in Madras, Bombay and Calcutta facilitated credit integration.[40]

Bombay's trade with the Deccan and Poona was conspicuous in its volume and value. Wars and political tension did not necessarily disrupt the commercial intercourse between Bombay and Poona—as the British Resident Charles Malet had more than one occasion to remark—and merchants found ways and means of bypassing blockages to direct their commercial ventures. Bombay's connection with Gujarat and Rajasthan tended to be even more solid given the importance of cotton as a staple export item in the trade of Calcutta and Bombay from where merchants re-exported the same to China. Thus the growing demand for cotton in China and the growing demand for the same staple in Bengal—a result of the Company's trade investments in textiles for the European market—coinciding with the rapid growth of English and European private trade in cotton produced a vigorous regrouping and reintegration of markets and networks.[41] Maratha cotton-bearing tracts in central India responded to the requirements of Calcutta and up-country north India triggering off the emergence of small towns. Dense urban clusters emerged in central India and the Awadh region—helping bankers and merchants to conduct their hundi operations with vigour and operate what was a dynamic and intermediate trading sector. On this was grafted the complex remittance network that serviced the rapid criss-cross movements of tribute transfers deployed by the Maratha and the English as well as the other regional powers.

The changing political context of transition thus constitutes the backdrop for the exploits of Trawadi Arjunji Nathji, the first protagonist—a key figure in the annals of business in western India. We shall have occasion to track his career and his business decisions as he emerged as the principal banker of the Company as it fought the Marathas to assume paramountcy over Hindustan. From his base in Surat he oversaw the growing density of credit and remittance operations in western India where all local powers took recourse to facilities extended by the bankers; he also benefited from the rising influence of the Company in western India, where after an initial period of slow and sluggish operations, it became a major player in the cotton and opium traffic with China, and also articulated its political aspirations with incisive clarity. By the end of Trawadi's lifetime the centre of political and commercial power in the region had shifted decisively to Bombay, where local merchants found new opportunities for business and profit. The situation was no longer that of tentative transition; by the first quarter of the nineteenth century the outlines of what one may call a 'colonial economy' had taken clear shape—endowing local merchants with a new set of challenges to respond to. Trawadi's last years coincided with the growth of Bombay as the trading emporium of western India and the ramifications of the region's trade in cotton and opium with China which were significant in expanding the business profile of the local merchants. The ambiguities of transition gave way to a more formalized regime of political control and economic domination, but with significant regional variations and inflections.

How would one define a colonial economy? Typically it was expected to function entirely to the advantage of the mother country—in this case, metropolitan Britain—and to that extent would certain mechanisms and procedures have to be in place in order to make economic extraction efficient. This involved both the allocation and appropriation of certain resources and the control of market processes.[42] Colonial economies were thus expected to provide raw materials for imperial economies and to be financially self-supporting so that the imperial economies did not have to siphon funds to keep the colonies intact. This logic meant that the colonial economy was characteristically export-oriented and was coerced into producing and delivering goods—mostly unprocessed and raw material—in order to balance the requirements of the imperial economy. During the next stage the colony was also expected to function as a captive market to absorb the manufactured goods of the metropolitan centre. In the case of India both these features gradually came into full focus by the first quarter of the nineteenth century as inevitable consequences of the Company's policies and because of the growing influence of private European and free trade interests that flocked to India in search of opportunities and markets. Without exaggerating the extent of the trade revolution engineered by the expanding English trading company it is important to note that the changes in demand, combined with conditions of political insecurity and conflict within the subcontinent and the Indian Ocean, did alter the context in which Indian traders had hitherto functioned. In fact Bombay's story of indigenous capital was largely scripted by the limits of the newly emerging colonial structure and not by its strength.

The transformation of the Indian trading economy occurred against the backdrop of major changes in Britain's trading interests and the growth of English private and free trade which affected the structure of the Company as well. As a chartered company it had enjoyed a virtual monopoly over trade between England and the East Indies (India and China included) while allowing licensed private merchants to carry on inter-Asian trading as well as inland trading within the subcontinent. The growing pressure from free traders in England as well as private traders in India—who were mainly ex-servants of the Company—ate into its monopoly, leading to a succession of Charter Acts (1813 and 1833) which, in the process, opened up a growing field for trade and investment.[43]

Two tendencies were at work in chipping away at the older contours of India's trading economy; one was the growing private trade of Company servants in India who began to invest in raw cotton, textile, and subsequently, opium, for the China market; and the other was the influx of British free traders into India who began to organize themselves into agency houses and invest in new export commodities for the larger global market. Both these developments were tied up with financing and remittance requirements of the Company which relied on private traders and bills to fund its trade to Britain. The complex enmeshing of private remittances with public transactions was evident in the way a new triangular trade relationship among India, China and Europe emerged, wherein India's status was decidedly subordinated to that of metropolitan Britain.[44] In the case of the English private merchants and British agency houses there was a growing interest and investment in raw cotton and opium exports to China—a development that helped the Company finance its official trade in Chinese tea.

After 1784, with the passing of the Commutation Act (introduced by William Pitt the Younger) that substantially lowered duties on tea imports, the Company relied not so much on bullion exports to finance tea purchases, as it did on Indian exports of cotton and opium. Returns on these exports solved the problems of remittance for the exporting private traders. The manner in which this worked was that at the level of matching supplies, Indian cotton and opium provided the necessary staple for securing tea consignments in China. These commodities also solved the problems of funding and remittance by integrating funds among Britain, India and China through bills of exchange in London and the Company's treasuries in India and Canton. Private merchants thus shipped opium and cotton to China, deposited the proceeds of their trade into the Company's treasury at Canton and in turn received bills of exchange drawn on the Company's treasuries in India or in London. In one smooth stroke the Company could access funds provided by private traders, and the latter could in turn use Company bills to transfer their profits to London without a fuss. This complex and innovative interlocking of financial and commercial interests began to dominate India's trading economy—producing an altogether unprecedented demand for cotton, opium and indigo that became crucial staples in supporting the channels of remittance.[45]

The implications of this were far-reaching. From being a producer of the cheapest textiles in Asia and a massive importer of silver, India rapidly became a dependent economy forced to turn over goods such as indigo, sugar, raw cotton and opium, and import vast amounts of manufactured goods from Britain.[46] Evidently this was a commercial revolution that had its share of casualties and beneficiaries. This revolution was largely spearheaded by European agency houses that from the 1780s began to directly intervene in the export–import trade, corner the trade in raw cotton and build an extensive business network from London. Their support was invaluable to the Company as they provided short-term cash during times of financial difficulty. In western India these houses worked closely with Indian partners who included Parsi merchants as well as merchants of mixed-Portuguese descent, and operated the raw cotton trade, even pushing the Bombay government to press for territorial expansion into the hinterland. What is thus striking about the western Indian story is the manner in which Indian merchants were able to work the newly emerging colonial economy to their advantage, even as older groups found it impossible to salvage their operations in a rapidly changing scenario. After 1812 when the doors of trade with China were thrown open a huge and expanding Chinese market for Indian opium provided an unprecedented opportunity for Bombay and its merchants. As Markovits writes, 'Between 1830–31 and 1860–61, the value of merchandise exported from Bombay increased sixfold and the value of opium exports increased tenfold'.[47] The opium connection, and tied to it, the remittance operations, gave merchants a huge range of commercial options, thus paving the way for substantial capital accumulation. The Parsi community in particular jumped into the fray from the very start and worked closely with the Europeans, the Company and the agency houses to emerge as one of the island city's most notable business communities. Their leading figure in the nineteenth century was the celebrated Jamsetjee Jeejeebhoy who entered into a partnership with Jardine Matheson, head of one of Canton's most powerful mercantile houses.

The travails of transition notwithstanding Indian traders and businessmen in western India were not shy of responding to new opportunities. If the Parsi community expanded their base as shippers and consignment merchants, the Banias, Gujaratis and Marwaris used the newly expanding communication channels to migrate outwards and emerge as massive financiers of cash crops. Their migration to central India peaked during the 1820s and coincided directly with the opium trade. The experience stood them in good stead for even after the decline of the opium traffic they were able to shift easily to the trade in cotton, grains and oilseeds.[48] The ability to function within interstitial spaces was what characterized the Bania enterprise; their sense of timing and willingness to take risk was what set them apart in a world of European domination. Whether it was Jamsetjee Jeejeebhoy or Premchand Roychand, the uncanny ability to foresee the advantages of the English connection was apparent. And nor was this purely instrumentalist in scope or sycophantic in its application. These were men who played for large stakes, invested in global commodity movements and participated in a changing public culture. Admittedly the logic and trajectory of Parsi business enterprise was not entirely comparable to that of traditional Bania enterprise, but what was striking was the way in which their location in Bombay city and its environment determined their business decisions.

The spectacular rise of Bombay as the financial capital of British India provided the backdrop for the extraordinary career of Premchand Roychand. Lured by the prospects of gain and profit the city became home to swathes of commercial migration, especially of Gujarati Banias. As early as the first quarter of the eighteenth century, communities of Gujarati Banias had made their way into the city, using to advantage the Company connection and its courts of justice. Like the Parsis they entered the service sector—acting occasionally as commission agents, trading in general merchandise as well as providing insurance and respondentia services to traders and exporters. They participated in the coastal trade, and with the cargo traffic to West Asia forged a link that was to expand even more greatly from the later decades of the nineteenth century. There were opportunities in abundance thrown up by the requirements of the Company for ships as well as for the city's provisioning, not to speak of cotton agencies. Just as the Wadia family[49] took to shipbuilding and dock-related services to establish a claim to the city's commercial space, so did Bania merchants enter the timber trade, working in collaboration with local and coastal merchants of Indian and hybrid extraction.

Their real break, however, came later in the eighteenth century and it was tied to the international trade dynamics of cotton. They experienced a windfall during the American Civil War when a disruption in Britain's cotton supplies caused a spiralling of cotton prices that lured Bania brokers and bankers to move into Bombay and operate its commerce. The resultant boom brought substantial wealth into Bombay—fuelling commodity, stock and real estate speculation, and brought to the fore, adventurers like Premchand Roychand—the third principal protagonist—a Surati Oswal and a cotton, bullion and stock trader. Anticipating later-day mavericks like Harshad Mehta by at least a century he demonstrated a daring and risk-taking disposition that stunned contemporaries who seemed to be always one step behind in the guessing game. Convincing the government and even senior bank officials to back his schemes Roychand showed an extraordinary ability to build around him a constituency of consenting collaborators. As an official inquiry report on the operations of the Bank of Bombay observed:

If Premchand had a friend to oblige, who wanted money he recommended him for a loan. If Premchand had shares to sell, he would suggest to an acquaintance that he should buy, offering at the same time to finance the purchase money, by procuring him a loan from the Bank of Bombay. If Premchand wanted money for speculation, he would suggest to some friend to join him in it, and then procure a loan in his friend's name for the money required. His influence was felt not only at the head office, but at the branches also, the agents at Kalbadevi, Broach and Surat all receiving instructions to consult Premchand or his agents respecting advances.[50]

Here was an evident case of charisma that persuaded men to trust him and believe in his dreams. As Wacha wrote:

Scores after scores of men would be seen in turn going in and out of the precincts of the bungalow, which was invariably accessible to all, the meanest as well as the most exalted, while at the door of the modest sanctum in which he held his levee might be seen batches of ten or more at a time waiting either for some business or another or allotment of shares.[51]

From the perspective of these merchants at least, the times were clearly exciting—fraught with tensions and risks, rich with possibilities of profit and prosperity and replete with challenges and prospects. It was a time for calculated risks, pragmatic alliances, reliable trust networks and quick reactions that had to be mediated through informal channels of funds and intelligence. Not only had alliances to be forged and firmed, business practices had to factor in new interventions in the forms of arbitration and adjudication. At the same time the merchants had to operate within certain constraints even in western India where the colonial state, in conjunction with European capital, held the reins of superior financial and technological power. It was here that two things helped: one was the enduring strength and importance of familial connections that guaranteed a measure of stability and security; and the other was the nature of the Indian bazaar which intersected in a complex way with the worlds of production and of distribution and connected the world of production with that of export trade.[52] The Company could not ignore the shroffs and local merchants, and even if their wings were clipped from time to time their centrality in servicing the complex systems of credit and exchange could hardly be undermined. From 1757 to 1857, in the long century of transition when the sovereignty of India changed hands, merchants came to occupy a very specialized role in transacting the business of state as well as in keeping intact the economy of circulation.

Without exaggerating the strength of Indian capital it is nonetheless worthwhile to understand its ramifications and its self-perception as it evolved over time and spilled into the public domain. Even as merchants accumulated and invested capital in lucrative ventures they assumed a new interest in a range of activities that may be loosely described as modern—encompassing philanthropic activities on the one hand and public welfare and municipal governance on the other. The confidence that the community gained was evident in the ways in which they set up businesses overseas and participated in complex citizenship narratives in the succeeding decades. They scripted new histories where a new mythology of mercantile success was assembled and which drew on an inheritance of shared success. Thus when Jeverilal Yajnik wrote to the editor of the *Bombay Gazette* in 1891, extolling the virtues of the Surat banker, Trawadi Arjunji Nathji whose house he likened to that of the Rothschilds', he did so with a shared sense of pride in a glorious mercantile past that required greater visibility and official recognition.[53]

And what was the attitude of the state to these traders and bankers? The issue is important given the conventional opposition posited between the ruler and the trader in Indian tradition and the so-called scriptural proscription against sea travel, as also the disdain shown to merchant culture by the landed aristocracy. Mughal culture was decidedly land-centred and oriented towards the ethos and etiquette of the landed elite and not so well disposed to the merchants or baqqals, whose influence in the century of Mughal decline came in for scathing criticism by contemporary chroniclers. The state, while conscious of the power that banking and mercantile communities enjoyed and the central role they played in sustaining treasury transfers as well as in expanding the cash nexus so crucial for the state's existence and expansion, was not especially generous in its disposition. This was a fact that European travellers were quick to comment on and in fact they exaggerated the lack of security of tenure under the imperial system. This misrepresentation discounted the more important set of arrangements that the state had in place and which could hardly be seen as anti-merchant.

On the contrary the state on the whole safeguarded merchant enterprise by building an efficient network of transport and communications. Confiscation of merchant property was by and large rare, and merchants were able to, and did, bequeath large fortunes to their successors, enabling family-firms to expand and thrive over generations. Given the absence of systemic and systematic state support, merchants tended to work through informal channels of leverage and relied on mechanisms like boycott when pushed to the wall or when their caste and social practices were infringed upon. It was this informality of association based on culture and caste that marked merchant ethos in the period under review and gave it depth and dimension to expand business ventures and respond to new stimuli. At the same time merchants rarely rejected state support outright; they watched the political situation with caution and introspection and hedged their bets in a way that gave them optimal advantage. This was evident time and again from the time of the Mughals to the 1857 revolt when merchants sized up their political patrons and distributed risks accordingly. During the great mutiny, bankers as a bloc tended to support the ruling administration which in their estimation was the right one as it offered and guaranteed financial security. The colonial state recognized this well; the magistrate of Allahabad once wrote to his superiors expressing his confidence in the mercantile classes who were solidly behind the British administration. The commissioner of Rohilkhand too had a similar opinion about those 'classes among the Hindoos who owe all they possess to the existence of the avowedly strongest and most just government . . . I mean the trading and banking class.'[54]

It must be kept in mind that the early colonial state and its working had benefited merchants and at the very least their immediate protégé financiers, thanks to the legal security guaranteed by the English authorities to debts and property and due to the newly emerging revenue arrangements that positioned the Bania favourably. Later too when the high imperial system was being consolidated in the course of the latter half of the nineteenth century with European firms extending their grip over commerce in the East and European exchange banks commanding the heights of the economy, the intermediation of the indigenous money and the supply market was critical. In Bombay the connections between the European and the indigenous sectors were even more visible as the state and European merchant interests maintained connections with indigenous capital.

At the same time such a concatenation of circumstances exposed the figure of the Bania merchant to easy stereotypes—stereotypes produced and perpetuated by the colonial discourse as a cringing loyalist and a cowardly and avaricious dealer. Yet neither the Bania merchant's support nor his apparent meekness could be taken for granted. He had recourse to go-slow tactics and the *hartal*—an effective weapon to bring the mighty to their knees—and had the appetite for risk-taking if dividends were large enough. Thus when J.N. Tata responded to the possibility of a national enterprise in steel, or Ghanshyam Birla to the call of Mahatma Gandhi, which offered possibilities of not just nationalist enthusiasm but real economic gain, there was no question of sitting on the fence. There was adventure to be sought, money to be made and a vision to be scripted.

Our protagonists, given their location in temporal and sociological terms, did not share the same vision but their lives and labour became legend. Trawadi Arjunji Nathji maintained and expanded a firm during a tumultuous period of India's history—battling against war, adversity, insecurity and fragmented authority. Jamsetjee Jeejeebhoy catapulted his community into an international league of business and enterprise, while Premchand Roychand emerged as a master of speculation even as he developed a more self-conscious appreciation of philanthropy and public service. Working within a complex environment these merchant princes did not merely rely on older strategies of community support but also developed a keen and measured appreciation for the new dispensation—investing in western education and its associated values that found expression in new modes of associational politics and recourse to new systems of law which seemed especially geared to the safeguarding of private property. None of the protagonists were especially concerned with the ethics of partnering the Company or the European private trader or, indeed, in the case of Jamsetjee Jeejeebhoy, pursuing traffic in a commodity such as opium that enslaved an entire nation. These were men of business who saw in the Company—dispensation, and in European collaboration—new sets of opportunities for investment and enterprise. They brought to bear their understanding of the market, of short-term risks, and developed a keen appreciation for new business opportunities that the nineteenth century brought in its wake. If Jamsetjee went out of his way to retain his associates' confidence in his activities, then Premchand was able to get away with audacious speculation that had the city in the midst of a share mania, followed by an equally spectacular crash. What was common to all of them was grit and resolve to confront adversity and to partake in the excitement that was almost contagious. In a century of transition replete with thrills and risks, traders and brokers became heroes as they emerged as major players not merely in a pan-Asian market but in an international one.

2. TRAWADI ARJUNJI NATHJI

THE 'HONOURABLE COMPANY'S SHROFF'

I do hereby declare that since my residence here as Chief of Surat, Tarwady Arjunji has always shown great attention and diligence for the interests of the Honourable East India Company and has by the transaction of his house as shroff rendered them every assistance and service in his power which at various times has been very essential.

—R.H. Boddam, Chief of Surat and Governor of Bombay, quoted in James Douglas, *A Book of Bombay*, 1883

BODDAM WAS NOT particularly original in his observations. The Surat banker Arjunji Nathji Trawadi had made an early impression on the servants and officials of the English East India Company as a crucial figure in the commercial world of western India in the second half of the eighteenth century. The banker's support and influence—materially in the form of hundis and loans, and morally in the form of sustained cooperation in the Company's quest for paramountcy—was seen as critical to the survival of the Company as a political and commercial aspirant in Hindustan. His career was in every sense the embodiment of the changes that the trading world of India registered in the fifty years of transition between two empires. His activity adjusted to the twists and turns of eighteenth-century politics, finding a niche in the complex web of political and commercial relationships that were continuously redrawn under the influence of rapidly changing political realities. His early career and fortunes were made in local and regional trade with his business operations moving along the trading axis of Benaras that connected the Gangetic plain with central and western India. His operations penetrated the web of financial transactions of local and regional powers—notably the chiefs of the Maratha Confederacy—and intersected the complex circuit of trading and commercial ventures that connected the western littoral region with the hinterland and with the West Asian economies. We do not have very clear and definitive dates for the banker's early life and operations, but it is evident that he was blessed with a long life which he spent in expanding his commercial and banking business, bankrolling the Company's political conquests in Hindustan, and in performing traditional caste-related functions—thereby creating for himself an image of a powerful philanthropist and merchant-magnate who could, if necessary, take even the law into his own hands. One can see how in 1800 following a case of murder in his household he was able to persuade the Company to adjudicate in his favour in accordance with caste-related principles and Brahmanical prescriptions rather than with the newly established tenets of the Company's law.

Trawadi Arjunji Nathji was a Nagar Brahmin from Surat whose family had ancestral connections with Benaras. His name occasionally crops up in early Company records; sometime in the 1740s he is referred to as a respectable merchant who was requested to act as an arbiter and adjudicator in a business dispute. Three years later he was identified as the Company's shroff in Surat.[1] This meant that he undertook the charge of the Company's local financial dealings, ensured deliveries of export consignments, and even interceded on its behalf when disputes arose with local merchants or rival companies. As a Nagar Brahmin his family was associated with trade and business and were respected for their integrity and enterprise—a reputation that persisted right through the nineteenth century evident from the nineteenth-century Nagar poets' reflections on the mercantile glories of Gujarat and its rich harvest of merchants and children of industry and enterprise. Trawadi Arjunji Nathji's family seems to have been based in Benaras in the eighteenth century when the city came under the influence of local rajas whose politics necessitated close links with mercantile and commercial groups. It is likely that Trawadi's family-firm also benefitted from the growth of Maratha political power and patronage in Benaras which helped it participate in the city's traffic in cotton and silk with western India. In fact the banker was very substantively involved in the silk traffic between Bengal and Surat and was found to belong to a cartel that monopolized this trade.[2] In accordance with custom and convention the family maintained agencies and branches in Gujarat whose operations generated handsome profits for the firm. In Surat Trawadi's firm was engaged in the city's extensive overseas trade which even after the spate of unrest during the eighteenth century continued to throw up prospects for gain. There are occasional allusions to the firm's dealings with merchants from West Asia and Arabs in particular,[3] although it would appear that by the 1750s the firm had definitely moved into the ambit of the Company—seen as a potential political patron. The reasons behind the choice were dictated purely by pragmatic considerations that characterized merchant behaviour at the best of times.

To locate the rise of the house of Trawadi Arjunji Nathji in the context of western Indian politics one must first of all identify the broad features of the political environment in which men like him had to operate. As mentioned briefly on an earlier occasion Surat for the greater part of the eighteenth century was forced to grapple with the pressures of political insecurity that accompanied the steady erosion of the Mughal political structure and the concomitant arrival of the Marathas in the region. For most Gujarati merchants and bankers, irrespective of religion and caste, the Maratha period in Gujarat's history was seen as, at least retrospectively, an unmitigated disaster. Given their attacks on the region's revenue base and their persistent demands on the city's revenue the local administration had little choice but to turn to their merchant subjects for financial 'assistance'. This frequently took the form of arbitrary taxes, the implications of which were particularly severe as they coincided with a commercial downturn. Faced with an impossible situation, the merchants toyed with the idea of aligning themselves with local powers which were seen as having the requisite leverage with the administration. This included the various European East India Companies that had since the seventeenth century maintained establishments or factories in the city, and had since then expanded their profile and portfolio by developing small, parallel centres of local patronage and jurisdiction. By the middle of the eighteenth century the European trading companies entered into semi-formal alliances with influential merchants and merchant groups to resist the ruling administration's demands especially in the matter of additional taxation.

The merchants of Surat had traditionally relied on a policy of maintaining informal connections with the Mughal provincial administration in the city, using these as levers to augment their trading prospects. Muslim merchants in the city appear to have enjoyed greater proximity to the Durbar although the commonality of interests based on religious affiliation must not be exaggerated. Some of the most influential merchants in the city happened to be Banias and Jains whose control over the money market was never seriously questioned by the state. However, following the decline of Mughal power in the first half of the eighteenth century, merchants were forced to look around for alternative sources of protection. The Company appeared to be the most viable source of protection. For one, they possessed naval strength that could be often deployed to harass the port authorities and impede day-to-day harbour operations and in the process enjoy a certain leverage in their negotiations with local officials. Further they were prepared to defend the claims of their client-merchants against the escalating demands of the local authorities. This became abundantly clear after the abortive merchant revolt of 1732[4] when the Surat merchants led by Mulla Muhammad Ali and the Company-backed Bania merchant Laldas Vithaldas Parekh, demanded the expulsion of Governor Sohrab Ali and his replacement by Teg Beg Khan as *mutasaddi* (senior Mughal official). The change of ruler, however, did not improve the situation and as the years rolled by the merchants became increasingly aware of the need to cement and formalize their connections with the Company. The realization was informed by the instances of the Company's support in claims of restitution and by the proactive role that the Company's broker Jagannathdas Laldas assumed in the 1750s.[5]

The English clique was one among many but arguably the most effective. One ought to consider that by the 1750s the power of the Dutch East India Company was on the wane and the increasing influence of English private trade enabled the Surat establishment of the Company to take the offensive in their negotiations with local officials. The decision therefore to align with the English circle was well calculated and gave the local Bania merchants the necessary breathing time to regroup and reorient their trading activities. By 1758 the decision to actually initiate a political revolution to elevate the Company into a formal position in the city's administrative set-up was taken and a coup d'état was set in motion. The occasion was the issue of succession to the office of the mutasaddi which was coveted by several officials. To neutralize the effects of succession-related wrangles and to forestall the disproportionate exercise of power by any one governor, the bankers of the city took the plunge. They met the Surat Council and proposed that the Company take up the position of qiladar and assume some degree of responsibility for the city's governance. They also pointed out in an important address that it was the only guarantor of security for their person and property that they would accept, for which they were prepared to commit a degree of financial support for a limited military campaign that the Company might consider. The bargain however, was to remain, understandably, a secret until the campaign was successfully executed. We do not at this stage hear anything about Trawadi or his involvement in the long and tortuous negotiations that led to the campaign in 1759, culminating in what is known as the Castle Revolution of 1759.[6]

The formal entry of the Company into the city's power structure was achieved with little effort. The naval force that set sail did not encounter serious opposition as both the local forces as well as the Maratha militia simply melted away. By a treaty signed with the ruling Nawab the English were appointed as qiladar and assumed joint responsibility for Surat thereby securing the right to appoint senior members of the administration and mediate in disputes with other European companies, the Nawab and other claimants as well as political aspirants. All these arrangements were endorsed by the Mughal authority in Delhi whose farman was received much later and at considerable expense. For this the credit goes to Trawadi whose influence in Delhi was evidently of some import. It was at this juncture that Trawadi emerged as a significant element in the changing power equations in the region. His decision to ally with the Company, like that of his counterparts, was informed by the conviction that the Company had the wherewithal to make good its debt obligations and that its political and military strength could be relied upon in times of need. His ability to negotiate on the Company's behalf with the Mughal authorities in Delhi was determined by the evident reputation his firm enjoyed as bankers and remitters, and their influence in the extensive inland trading network which despite the political crisis held fast and remained functional. In fact it was the continuing importance of the east–west axis of the subcontinental trade between Bengal and Surat via Benaras and Awadh which constituted the material base of indigenous banking activity in India in the second half of the eighteenth century.

The importance of Trawadi's banking house is part of a larger history of Indian banking that expanded quite substantially in this transitional period, largely in the wake of regional political consolidation spearheaded by powers like the Marathas, the kingdom of Awadh, the Raja of Benaras, and the new power: the Company based in Calcutta. Political consolidation generated its own demands for remittances of funds across treasuries and tribute-receiving units and at the same time fostered conditions for inland trade and pilgrimage which was an important adjunct to trade as is evident in the case of Benaras and the religious fair of Haridwar. Historians have noted the importance of pilgrimage-related income and ritual movements in sustaining the overall unity of the Indian trading and banking economy.[7] We know how pilgrims from Gujarat, Maharashtra and Bengal took credit notes and bills from their local bankers to have them cashed by Benaras bankers and how this constituted a major source of capital deposit for the Bania banking community. For the greater part of the second half of the eighteenth century the radiating effects of regional politics—especially that of the Maratha Confederacy—and the strains and pulls of the Company-dominated trading poles of Calcutta, Bombay and Madras on the banking and credit networks in northern, central and western India were evident. The rise and success of Trawadi Arjunji Nathji testified to this new configuration of trade and politics that gave the Gujarati Brahmin banker an extensive field and diverse portfolio to play with.

Some of the options that were available to this young man in the decades after the Castle Revolution of 1759 are detailed below. One must keep in mind that the reconstruction of his business dealings is entirely based on contemporary references in official documentation of the Company with all its expected biases. It is likely that regional and vernacular sources alluding to Trawadi's financial dealings would have had a different slant but there is little doubt that his extensive dealings with the Company or his orientation to the Company dispensation would have gone unnoticed. In the official records of the Company he is almost always identified as their most important and principal shroff, assuming responsibility for its requirements and facilitating its transactions with other

bankers and merchants in the city as well as with other
political claimants. This position was a direct consequence of
Arjunji's decision to stand firmly behind the Company in its
capacity as the most serious political contender in the region.
This did not however, preclude his dealings with other local
powers—including the Maratha Confederate chiefs—whose
requirements for financial and remittance facilities were met
by him as well as by other local bankers.

Apart from the all-important business of state-financing,
Trawadi was extensively involved in the region's silk trade
with Benaras as well as in the textile and cotton trade in
western India, which fed into the remittance and credit
networks that the Company and other regional powers dipped
into. The Company on its part was unstinting in its support
to the banker. In 1759 he was invited to send an agent and set
up shop in the city of Bombay even as he was appointed the
Company's treasurer in Surat. As head of a senior business
firm in Bombay, Arjunji not only deployed the Company
connection to expand his trade dealings with local and overseas
merchants—by using the Company's convoy protection for
bullion consignments that came from overseas into Bombay
and Surat—but also intervened to systematize commercial
practices especially during moments of contestation and legal
disputes. What is apparent and impressive is the way his
reputation as an honourable merchant for whom reciprocal
trust and honour (abru) were of paramount importance
became a benchmark that was cited in legal cases that appeared
before the Mayor's Court in Bombay. He was frequently
invited to both—give evidence in particular cases and

deliberate on issues relating to the interpretation of specific customs and commercial practices.[8]

A typical working day in the life of Trawadi Arjunji would have been something like this. In Surat he resided at the Balajichakla—one of the commercial localities that bankers and Bania merchants resided in—he would begin his day by checking his accounts and deposits carefully recorded in the *bahi*s or account books which were kept in safe custody. These deposits came from a variety of sources indicating the diversity of his portfolio, from local citizens including the assets of widows and other women, merchants, traders, revenue farmers as well as government officials. The scrutiny would be followed by a careful consideration of investments, textile and silk purchases, and loans and credit assistance given to the local merchants. He was a senior farmer of customs revenue (*mokatee*) from silk in Surat.[9] He also extended credit to local powers—the ruling Muslim administration, the Maratha revenue officials stationed in Surat and the Company. A considerable time was spent in ensuring that correspondence and records were intact and in going through news from agents in Gujarat who were engaged in the business of brokerage and banking in Bombay and Benaras. On this depended the success and efficacy of Trawadi's business and the vitality of the remittance network. He visited the local revenue office on a daily basis to check on his share of the *mokat*s that represented town duties on imports entering the city and which were generally farmed out to the highest bidder. He would also regularly visit the Company factory to keep abreast of developments there.

Consultations and a close watch over the money market constituted a part of his regime. Often he was called upon to assist with inquiry commissions that the Company set up to investigate the state of the money market, coinage and other related business matters; he would also make visits to Bombay when his expert counsel was needed on matters related to insurance- and brokerage-related practice. That his counsel and stature were acknowledged is amply clear from the cases in the Mayor's Court where he was often asked to comment on the validity of a certain set of practices over another.

The banker seems to have maintained a large establishment in Surat. Though there are no clear details of his establishment in Surat, what seems reasonably clear on the basis of reconstruction is that he supported a sufficiently large contingent of servants, security personnel, agents and peons to assist him in his affairs. This was conditioned largely by the need for confidentiality and to ensure the security of the assets that he maintained in the form of cash, jewels, and account registers and books. Further the acceleration in the pace of business activities especially in the wake of the Company's political expansion in western India and its rivalry with the Maratha power in the region meant that the banker had to travel extensively to oversee his various branch offices or kothis, dispersed across the subcontinent, as well as maintain regular correspondence with a network of reliable agents and subordinates whom he chose and trained with care. Mulchand Dube and Arat Ram Tiwari for example were close confidantes who maintained regular contacts with their employer when they had cause to attend on the

Company in Calcutta, Murshidabad and Benaras—tending to its requirements for cash and credit. As a political aspirant and a major player of international trade the Company in its official and private capacity required extensive local or indigenous financial support for a variety of reasons, and bankers like Trawadi exploited this to their advantage.

From the 1770s the situation both in Surat (where Trawadi was based) and in western India began to show signs of change triggered largely by the growing ambitions of the Company. By this time three developments had played themselves out. One was the consolidation of the Company's power in Bengal and its growing penetration into the state of Awadh that took the form of escalating revenue demands— ostensibly to support a subsidiary military force which it cobbled together and stationed in Awadh as a guarantee for peace and to safeguard its interests. This was met by periodic remittances that were funnelled largely through the local credit networks that Trawadi Arjunji Nathji operated together with Benaras bankers and Lucknow firms such as those of Lala Kashmiri Mal. Secondly there were the signs of a clear-cut political agenda wherein the Company authorities in Bombay wished to carve a sphere of influence in Gujarat by engaging the Marathas. The choice of Gujarat was predictable; it was an export-rich region yielding cotton, and European and Parsi merchants who traded in raw cotton there urged the Company authorities to safeguard their interests; this inevitably led to greater political control over the area and deeper financial collaboration with local bankers and brokers. Thirdly there was a growing realization among indigenous bankers that associating with the Company was the safest political alternative. Not surprisingly banking houses like the firm of Trawadi Arjunji Nathji emerged as major financiers and bankers for the Company and supported them especially during times of war. Admittedly like good merchants whose ventures were determined by a measure of pragmatism the bankers maintained strong links with local powers including the Marathas; but what is worthy of notice is the precedence that the Company enjoyed in their calculations and estimation and how their special relationship with the Company was factored in by the other powers. The intimacy of the Company's connections with the banker came into focus especially during and after the First Maratha War. A letter penned by Trawadi Arjunji illustrates this rather quaintly. In an epistle dated 24 July 1793 he informed the Company at Fort William that he had recently been to Baroda where Manaji Rao Gaekwad, son of Damaji Rao Gaekwad, 'showed him great kindness as hospitality, which, he is sure, was due to his connection with the Company'. The writer stayed there for some days and at the time of his departure 'Manaji Gaekwad earnestly expressed his wish to cultivate friendship with the English and desired him therefore to put in touch with his lordship.'[10]

What this missive demonstrates—besides the obvious regard the banker had for the English elaborated in a ritually ornate style meant for public display as much as for private communication—is the astute assessment of the power of the Company whose intercession was sought after by many of the local powers in the subcontinent and in which the banker was willing to play the role of a broker. The letter also included the banker's advice to the Company to dispatch a suitable letter to Manaji Rao Gaekwad, on the receipt of which the latter would send 'a reply and a vakil and a suitable nazrana and will thereby manifest his obedience and submission to the Company'.[11]

The years leading to the First Maratha War and thereafter were marked by subtle shifts in the Company's political project as well as the Marathas who were responding to the changes that characterized the politics of this period. In terms of the broader politics of the subcontinent the 1770s saw dissensions developing within the Maratha Confederacy that continued to be the alternative power centre in the subcontinent. In their reinvented form after the Third Battle of Panipat in 1761 the Marathas had consolidated their respective special zones of influence—the Gaekwads in Baroda, the Holkars in Indore, and the Sindhias in Malwa, central India and Gujarat, along with interests in Delhi. The Marathas also continuously adjusted and altered their relations with the Company whose competing claims were seen as expressions of hostility. The other regional powers like the Nizam of Hyderabad or the Nawab of Awadh were operating under a reduced status as quasi-subsidiary allies of the Company, and with the exception of Mysore that foiled the Company's claims in southern India, most of them operated as lukewarm contenders for supremacy and fair-weather friends of any power under consideration. What integrated the politics of all these powers was the credit network that channelled funds for both trade and war, with battles being fought in dispersed theatres. More locally, in western India, the Marathas remained wary of the Company's presence despite the precarious state of the Company's finances in Bombay. This created, almost by default, an overwhelming dependence on the hundi network that the English authorities of Fort William used to transport funds and subsidies to their counterparts in Bombay. Thus from the very outset it was evident that any major political project in western India would require the support of indigenous bankers—a feature that worked with demonstrable effect during the First Maratha War. Meanwhile the situation in Gujarat, specifically in Surat, deteriorated as far as municipal order was concerned—something that the banking community could only view with concern and apprehension. Under the circumstances it was not entirely surprising that Trawadi should emerge as a major protagonist of the Company and exercise pressure on its authorities to fulfil their obligations when it came to his own settlement claims or credit-related demands. The banker did not shy away from making public his expectations from the Company whether for private ends—like guarantees for safe trips—or for commercial bargains. This was derived from the pre-eminence that the Trawadi house began to enjoy from about the late eighteenth century in the field of remittances and which determined the scale and success of the Company's operations.

It was during the First Maratha War that the hundi factor became critical for the Company. The events leading up to the conflict were informed by the Company's resolve to develop Bombay's maritime hinterland by annexing the contiguous islands of Salsette, Bassein, Elephanta, Karanja and Hog so as to neutralize the Maratha influence along the coast as well as to expand the Company's control over the cotton-rich territories in south Gujarat and Kathiawar where the influence of the Maratha chiefs—the Sindhias and the Gaekwads—prevailed.[12] Meanwhile succession disputes at the centre of Maratha power in Poona, in the wake of Peshwa Madhav Rao's death, encouraged the Bombay Council to step in. Raghunath Rao, one of the key claimants, was ordered to leave Poona on charges of high treason and murder when he approached the Company authorities in Bombay for help. The council responded with alacrity as it saw in this an opportunity to press claims upon the adjacent islands. On 6 March 1775 the Bombay Council concluded the Treaty of Surat whereby it promised 225 English troops to help Raghunath Rao recover lost ground and his *masnad* (throne) in Poona. On his part, Raghunath Rao or Raghoba, promised the islands of Salsette and Bassein as well as a sum of Rs 6 lakh to defray the expenses of the expedition. These arrangements proved to be premature as the Calcutta Council roundly condemned the treaty, questioning the right of Bombay to conduct independent diplomacy without its final approval. In 1775 the Treaty of Surat was abandoned in favour of a new one, the Treaty of Purandhar. In accordance with the terms of the new agreement peace was restored on the payment of Rs 12 lakh. The cause of Raghoba was all but jettisoned until the Court of Directors in London approved a military offensive. The Surat treaty came into force with financial arrangements in place for the Company forces to fight the war. As it happened the war yielded little tangible benefits but it demonstrated the capabilities of the Surat bankers, notably Trawadi Arjunji Nathji, as the major financiers of the Bombay government whose support could be mobilized whenever necessary and could be counted upon at all times.

The Bengal–Benaras–Surat network of remittances came into its own even as armies of the Company marched rather desultorily against their Maratha opponents up-country. Remittances to the tune of nearly Rs 15 lakh were made to Bombay in January 1780 in order to help defray the expenses of the army under General Goddard who used his discretion in contracting supplies from the Surat bankers, notably Trawadi Arjunji and Atmaramdas Bhucandas among others.[13] It was a testing time for bankers who had to calculate the risks involved in salvaging their commercial operations and diverting funds to the war effort. Trawadi Arjunji seems to have taken a risk as he was aware of the necessity for hundi transfers and of the advantages he enjoyed from the larger banking fraternity, not to mention the dividends he derived from the Surat–Bengal traffic. By 1782 when the Treaty of Salbai was signed to enforce peace between the two contenders the importance of the hundi and the influence that Trawadi Arjunji wielded in the money market was evidence enough to convince the Company of the necessity of keeping the banker on its side. It now remained for the Company to work closely with its principal banker who exhibited his astute business acumen in extracting the best terms for his business while remaining steadfast behind the Company's political project. The Company had no alternative but to treat Trawadi Arjunji with deference notwithstanding its extreme indignation as is evident from its annual reports about the manipulative tendencies of indigenous bankers and merchants. Some attempts to curb his influence or that of the Benaras banking house of Gopaldas Manohardas were not effective. For instance in 1788–89 tenders for remittance services were accepted by bankers such as Kelbjee Telookjee who agreed to a lower exchange rate between the Bengal and the Bombay Rupee, and the government saw it as an opportunity to keep the big bankers in check. An extract from a letter reveals: 'The innovation is of course not agreeable to the three or four principal bankers, who heretofore have been the channels of the said remittances and they accordingly did at first join in refusing to reduce rates, in consequence this tender by the house of Kelbjee Telookjee will ultimately oblige the other houses to be more reasonable in their charges'.[14] The letter also proceeded to mention that almost immediately, Arat Ram Tiwari, the *gomasta* (clerk) of Arjunji Nathji Trawadi was prepared to negotiate at a reduced rate of 7 per cent.[15]

Unfortunately for the Company this optimism was short-lived as it was forced to realize that without the sustained support of the big men its requirements could not be met. Thus by 1790 it was evident that the entire business of servicing the requirements of the Company by providing its forces with money when required or facilitating remittances between the Company's treasuries to maintain its respective establishments were shared by the house of Trawadi Arjunji and the Benaras banking firm of Gopaldas Manohardas.

What made such an extraordinary cartel possible? Sources reveal that Trawadi Arjunji Nathji was in a position to command the deposits and savings of smaller bankers which he subsequently invested in extensive cross-country trade and remittances. The sheer scale of the Company's requirements during war and peace required the commanding presence of a banker like Trawadi Arjunji Nathji who could, at short notice, guarantee large supplies. Consequently he could demand favourable terms for his services. This was possible due to the network of trust and reciprocity that he had built through a carefully constituted structure of agents and managers, on the basis of his reputation for absolute punctuality and creditworthiness—all this stood him in good stead especially during a period when remittances drove the local, regional and larger pan-Indian economy. Choosing the Company as patron was probably the most pragmatic decision that the banker undertook—realizing fully well that its emphasis on property rights and business practices facilitated his ventures. At the same time he was able to drive a hard bargain exploiting the Company's locational disadvantages in wartime and in an era of transition.

The political project of the Company especially in western India was hamstrung by several factors. The fragile financial basis of the Company in Bombay was a major constraint. Until the later decades of the eighteenth century Bombay's survival as a Company settlement was in serious doubt. Lacking territory as well as revenue from land and customs duties the Bombay government was almost entirely dependent on local bankers and on the support of the Fort William authorities who remitted funds through indigenous credit networks operated by local bankers. At the same time the fact that India did not have a uniform legal tender in circulation meant that the expertise of shroffs who knew the differential exchange rates between various types of currencies became critical in arranging for remittances to pay the army and its commanding officers. This became especially crucial when wars and campaigns were fought in discrete and dispersed theatres and when supplies had to be bought with local currency. This feature came up in sharp focus during the Second Maratha War that decisively established the Company's influence in western India, and Trawadi Arjunji as its most 'honourable shroff'.

Between 1782 and 1803 Trawadi Arjunji Nathji steadily built up his assets and proximity to the Company. It is likely that he invested in the raw cotton trade that was becoming important for the western Indian economy. He also continued to develop substantial interests in the Surat–Bengal trade in cotton and silk—which happened to constitute the principal conduit of remittance between Bengal and western India. His influence would no doubt have penetrated the inland trade in cotton and opium with central India that John Malcolm, as resident of Malwa, had occasion to speak of. While Malcolm did not specify Trawadi the Surat banker his account indicates how extensive and interconnected the money market and inland trade was. Commenting on the large traffic for hundis in central India, he observed:

> An amount of two to three lacs monthly is drawn from Mhow and Indore in bills on the treasuries of the

western provinces of Hindustan, and there can be no doubt that nearly double that sum may be negotiated at a favourable rate of exchange at the cities of Oojein and Indore. The provinces of Central India send rich produce to Gujarat and the Deccan, but export few articles to Hindustan, and to Mirzapore, from whence a great proportion of their imports are received . . . add to this that the bankers and agents of Oojein and Indore are often the medium of the Gujarat payments for the merchandise from the Bengal provinces. There is still another cause; a great number of natives of the Company provinces are in service, or have become inhabitants of Central India. These continually require remittances and have usually recourse to petty shroffs or money lenders, who engage to pay money to their families at their place of residence.[16]

Given the persaviness of hundi transactions, it is easy to understand how Trawadi Arjunji Nathji's extensive commercial operations fitted into the logic of existing business and financial arrangements. What was impressive was the manner in which the banker managed to maintain his pre-eminent position in the remittance business, the scrupulous way he augmented his reputation and contacts, the keeping of close tabs on his agents in Calcutta, and travelling as extensively as possible to his various offices. This required great personal energy and supervision and one gets glimpses of both from contemporary records. He used his connections with the Company to get favourable interviews with other regional powers and chieftains, and also for safe passage during trade and personal trips. We have a letter from the banker to the British governor-general in 1795 stating that Ratan Chand—his gomasta and successor to his old and trusted agent Mulchand—wished to go to Benaras 'to celebrate the marriage of his sons and also to settle there for the rest of his life leaving the business to someone else and that the new man should enjoy the same confidence and respect that his predecessor had always enjoyed', requesting at the same time a safe passage to Benaras, which he hoped the Company could guarantee by writing to the Maratha power that enjoyed special influence in the pilgrim city.[17]

What emerges from a careful reconstruction of official Company documentation of the period is the solidity of the banker's investment in a long-term relationship with the Company, the steady consolidation of assets through careful management and the maintenance of community ties. These became key factors in the extraordinary pre-eminence and success of the house of Trawadi Arjunji Nathji especially in the first decades of the nineteenth century when Bombay made a serious and substantive bid for political power. The extent of the banker's credit came into full focus in the opening years when a series of major wars was fought between the Company and the Marathas, wherein the local merchants had high stakes.

By 1800 the Company had secured full control over Surat city by initiating a number of administrative and judicial arrangements, the execution of which enjoyed the tacit support of the city's senior merchants like Trawadi. By this time there was hardly any doubt that the Company intended to assume substantive powers in the city where municipal administration had virtually collapsed—rendering business and other quotidian functions impossible. The city saw two major riots in 1788 and 1795, although in both these instances the property of Trawadi Arjunji Nathji was not targeted or attacked. Almost every month there were petty altercations between the lower echelons of the ruling administration and the clients of the Company, including supervising officers at the Company's custom house, known as 'the Latty'. All this disrupted commercial operations and increased the sense of insecurity among the local merchants. Under these circumstances it was not surprising that the commercial groups in Surat, especially the Banias and Parsis, continually and persistently solicited the Company to assume real power and dislodge the ruling Nawab from his position. This coincided with growing apprehensions of the Bombay merchants (Europeans and Parsis) about lawlessness and predation along the coast that threatened to affect their cotton ventures. Consequently they mounted pressure on the Company to take the offensive in the western littoral and in Gujarat thereby feeding into the larger political project of the Company.

The key to the successful implementation of this project was of course finance and its availability in the multiple theatres of war and aggression. Initially the Bombay government attempted to look beyond its local collaborators and financiers and approached European merchants and agency houses for assistance, and even found it for a brief period in the form of the Forbes Loan and of public subscriptions.[18] However, neither of these proved sufficient to carry out the expenses of war and so Trawadi Arjunji Nathji once more stepped forward to finance the Company's wars. The negotiations leading to the financial arrangement entered into with the banker demonstrated how he actively dominated the money market and was able to drive out all competition. His contract promised regular supplies of money to the Bombay government and the army.[19]

Almost immediately after the outbreak of war there was a scramble for mobilization of fiscal resources which was needed to effectively fight a set of dispersed campaigns. It became important for the Company to capitalize on the relative financial disarray in the Maratha camp as well as to ensure that the support of the more affluent shroffs was firmly yoked to the Company. The importance of controlling the money market was not lost on the Company and this in turn became a major advantage for bankers who were able to dictate their terms.

In 1803 negotiations were afoot for a contract that would specify the terms on which Trawadi would advance money to the Company. These were tedious and protracted as the banker insisted on certain conventions for discounting hundis, while the Company still toyed with the possibility of bypassing Trawadi entirely and entering into an agreement with smaller bankers who would agree to discount Surat bills at par with local currencies which were required to provision the marching armies. However, Trawadi was able to summon his influence to deter smaller shroffs from agreeing to any proposal made by the Company, and so eventually by 1804 contracts were drawn out with the banker stipulating the amount to be paid and the logistics to be adopted for facilitating its transmission.[20] It is interesting to note that during this period when there was a flurry of financial activity, with the government floating a public loan for subscriptions, and the Bombay agency houses—principally led by Forbes and Company and Fawcett and Company—agreeing to deposit in the Company's treasury a stipulated sum to be adjusted against licenses to purchase cotton as well as against the Company's treasury bills, Trawadi Arjunji Nathji maintained a low profile stepping in only when the European loans proved insufficient and when other bankers withdrew from the scene. It needs to be borne in mind here that from 1800 there were a number of merchant bankruptcies in Surat and there was a contraction in the inland trade between central and western India whose repercussions were shouldered by several bankers. How and why Trawadi Arjunji Nathji escaped this fate is not entirely clear; one can only speculate that he had gained sufficient influence to provide the finances and that his connection with the Company had enabled him to make good his investments. For instance as the Company expanded its influence in the regional political structures like the one in Baroda, Trawadi Arjunji's banking house followed suit as it successfully assumed charge of receiving the state's revenues and remitting the share due to the Company through its channels. The pan-India ramifications of his firm made it possible for Trawadi to operate as the principal conduit for the Company's financial processes. His credit reputation and his influence over the money market made him an invaluable ally whom the English could hardly discount. The high point of his partnership thus came in 1804 when he came forward to sign the Bombay Contract with the Company by which he agreed to provide necessary sums to the armies fighting in various parts of central India. A brief outline of the contract and its context is useful to illustrate the ramifications and dimensions of Trawadi Arjunji Nathji's support and how central it was for an army fighting a series of desperate campaigns.

In 1800 the Company, inspired by the imperialist vision of Lord Wellesley, decided to embark upon a major campaign against the Marathas—its principal opponent in western and central India, who enjoyed influence in the Ganga–Yamuna Doab, the bread basket of India that had been coveted by successive powers. The cause for intervention was provided by dissensions within the Maratha camp thanks to the hostility that subsisted between the Peshwa ruler in Poona and the chiefs of confederacy dynasties like the Sindhias, Bhonsles and Holkars, who each commanded their respective spheres of influence. The Company authorities targeted the weak Peshwa who was willing to side with the English against his confederate chiefs, and the result was the Treaty of Bassein which was concluded on 31 December 1802. In accordance with its terms the Peshwa was promised English protection in exchange for a subsidy of Rs 26 lakh assigned for the maintenance of a British army in his territories. He was forbidden to enter into any diplomatic relations with a third power without the concurrence of the Company.

The treaty was short-lived. The senior chiefs of the Maratha Confederacy rejected it outright and inevitably the scene was set for a confrontation. This time the campaigns were not concentrated in any single theatre of battle. The focus of the northern campaign was on seizing control over Delhi, Agra and the Doab, while the Deccan campaign was on securing vital areas like Ahmednagar. Besides, supplementary campaigns were planned to seize valuable territory in Gujarat and central India. In 1803 Governor-General Wellesley outlined a very specific set of objectives in a dispatch to Lord Lake: one, to seize all the territories belonging to the confederate's senior leader Daulat Rao Sindhia in north India; two, to form an alliance system with the Rajputs and rulers of other smaller states in the west of Delhi; and three, to occupy the territory of Bundelkhand. The sphere south of the Narmada river was entrusted to Colonel Wellesley who was instructed to advance to the Peshwa's capital in Poona, receive the Peshwa, Baji Rao II, and promote his cause. The Bombay army on the other hand was given orders to march against Sindhia's power in Gujarat, strike at his possessions in Broach and make a bid for the cotton-yielding territories in the region. The Madras army was organized under the leadership of Colonel Murray and Colonel Stuart who were expected to strike at and annihilate the Gaekwads' power in Baroda. The core force remained under the charge of Lord Lake who was ordered to confront Sindhia in north India and to seize his possessions between the Ganga and Yamuna rivers, to bring back Emperor Shah Alam to Delhi under the umbrella of British protection, and to form alliances with local powers like the Rajputs thereby isolating their principal adversary, the Sindhias. The dispersed nature of the campaigns was a huge challenge as it required careful supervision of supplies and accessibility of funds in order to keep the military contented. Funds had to be channelled and transferred punctually and made available in the local currency which would enable easier provisioning. This was not as easy as it seemed—the circulation of different local currencies meant that precise calculations had to be made about the exchange rates between Surat rupees and Jaipur or Ujjain rupees as the case might be. This applied to hundis as well—discount rates had to be specified. In the circumstances, relying on ad hoc arrangements or on fly-by-night operators was not an option. Both the Company as well as its rivals realized the importance of fiscal support, and it was here that Trawadi Arjunji Nathji's support and intervention became so critical. For this reason his ability to command the money market and side consistently with the Company became so decisive in determining the success of the English. The money market thus emerged as the real site of power as the English and Maratha competed to control it through their respective banking partners. The Company tried to maintain some kind of leverage on the banker but this proved to be more ritualistic than real. Indeed the negotiations between the Company and the Surat shroff revealed at every stage the obvious bargaining strength the latter possessed.

The first enactment of the banker's strength was in 1803 and revolved around the wording and interpretation of the contract finalized between the Company with Trawadi. The terms of the contract specified that Trawadi would pay into the Company's treasury for the regular provisioning of

Colonel Murray's army.[21] Differences arose over exchange rates and the interpretation of hundi conventions regarding payment.[22] There were two principal conventions in vogue: the *Hundi Ritt Roka* and the *Hundi Ritt Atna*—the first requiring payment in the current coin of the place on which the hundi was drawn without regard to exchange, whereas in the second case it was understood that for every 100 rupees at the place where the hundi was drawn, there was to be a corresponding flat payment of 109 rupees, irrespective of the exchange rate. The Surat banker insisted on the latter convention, much to the Company's annoyance. In September 1803 the Company got in touch with other local bankers[23] and tried to persuade them to enter into an agreement on more favourable terms. However, the influence of Trawadi deterred the smaller bankers from agreeing to the proposal, with the result that the coveted contract reverted to Trawadi. A compromise was reached—a fresh contract in which Trawadi the banker was expected to pay a monthly sum of Rs 7 lakh which would be exchanged at par with local currency in the areas north of the Narmada including Broach. For the south of the Narmada a different agreement was reached, and Trawadi was allowed to receive bills at Surat when these were presented within eight days on receipt at the rate of 102 Surat rupees for every 100 rupees. The banker argued that the unfavourable exchange rate with Baroda had exposed him to great risk and expense and that it was with great difficulty that he had been able to provide for the British detachment. In a letter to Jonathan Duncan on 3 August 1804 he stated that the unfavourable rate of exchange was affecting his interests adversely and fervently hoped that some concessions would be forthcoming for his troubles.[24]

However, the Company held its ground, refusing to accommodate the banker's demands. This impasse did not help matters and almost immediately the Company representatives in Surat informed their superiors in Bombay that Trawadi Arjunji's refusal had hardened the attitude of other shroffs who declared themselves entirely unwilling to carry out such a transaction. Negotiations were resumed with the banker and a contract was finally drawn up at the end of the month under which Arjunji Trawadi agreed to provide on a monthly basis, a sum of Rs 60,000 for the provisioning of the Bombay troops camped in Malwa and elsewhere. For every 100 rupees provided in camp in the approved local currency he was to receive 110 Surat rupees payable half in cash at Baroda and the other half by bills on Benaras, Lucknow and Calcutta, i.e., all the treasuries in whose operations Trawadi had a share. The banker also insisted on enjoying a monopoly over such remittance-related services. The contract remained in force but not without hitches, and, much to its annoyance, entailed the ultimate submission on the part of the Company. As the accountant-general of the Company in the Bombay establishment observed it was impossible to gauge or estimate the fair rate of exchange between different circulating currencies in view of the huge and inflated demand for money required in the various military camps. In his words, 'The magnitude of the required supply so far exceeds what is usually so by individuals for remittances by Hoondy that no fair comparison can be made of the current rates.'[25]

In short what the accountant-general emphasized in a long and tedious report was that Trawadi's contract was indispensable and for the sake of prosecuting the mammoth war effort, the temporary inconvenience of harsh terms was to be suffered. Trawadi Arjunji too resisted compromise as far as the exchange rate was concerned even as he used the opportunity to consolidate his control over the business of treasury transfers. Time and again when differences surfaced on the issue of exchange and discount the old banker insisted on his interests being safeguarded by the Company. The authorities in Bombay who were more familiar with the local situation were more responsive to Arjunji Trawadi's demands even if these did not go down well with the superior authorities in Fort William.

By and large the contract worked satisfactorily even though minor complaints about punctuality arose from time to time. On virtually every occasion the Company was careful not to test the shroff's patience and thus tried to ensure by every means possible that the army was supplied with cash. In February 1805 the Bombay government expressed its hope that Trawadi Arjunji would continue to supply funds and even promised him a *khilat*, or robe of honour if he so complied with his agreement. Trawadi kept his commitments but rarely yielded on the issue of exchange rates or protocols of payment. In 1805 the Bombay government informed the Company's agents at Surat that it had agreed to accept Trawadi Arjunji's contract wherein he was expected to remit Rs 6 lakh on the first of every month, and to respond to the paymaster's demands at different stations within Gujarat; and in return he would receive bills on Surat payable at par except in the case of Surat itself, wherein the banker would receive for every 100 Bombay rupees, 102 Surat rupees.[26]

The signing of the contract did not necessarily iron out mutual differences; at every stage the banker tried to extract more advantages while the Company resisted. For instance in 1805 he mentioned that his agent Dulabdas along with Elphinstone had fixed the Jaipur rate of exchange at Rs 15 (i.e., the amount that a certain number of Surat rupees would earn in the Jaipur coin) and he had no prior intimation of this and it that would injure his interests almost to the tune of Rs 2 lakh. In his opinion the exchange rate had to be increased to Rs 17. The Bombay authorities resisted this suggestion arguing that the actual money never went beyond Baroda and so the question of an escalating exchange rate did not arise. The negotiations persisted until Trawadi Arjunji wrote to the Bombay government saying that while he was prepared to furnish Rs 16 lakh at a difference of Rs 15, the rest could only be given at a difference of Rs 17. He also drew attention to the vast amount of funds that remained unpaid and the fact that he did not wish to receive as payment, bills on Calcutta as these had been transacted at a loss. He concluded by saying that unless his suggestions were taken seriously he would be in trouble and he would not be able to 'procure funds in Surat as the shroffs do not take any bills on Calcutta that I would gather funds notwithstanding'.[27] The Company in spite of its initial reservations gave in, for it realized all too well the critical nature of the banker's support.

As it happened Trawadi Arjunji Nathji was fully aware of

the advantages of his position: as a senior shroff who controlled the pan-Indian credit network, he alone had the staying power to support the Company's escalating demand for bills. This not only gave him access to a range of ancillary business activities that helped in the expansion of his firm it also gave him enormous local power and influence that he could deploy whenever necessary. In fact before the Second Maratha War (1803–1805) as the first citizen of the old city of Surat he was able to hold his own in matters of private management even if these went against the Company's notions of public justice. Nowhere was this more graphically demonstrated than by the famous trial of 1800 involving the senior banker in a case of manslaughter. What is fascinating about the case and its resolution is the nature and mode of negotiation between early colonial rule (represented by the Company) and indigenous capital (represented by the banker). It reveals how early colonial rule accommodated traditional notions of caste and honour that buttressed the loyalty of indigenous capital towards imperial expansion and how indigenous commercial groups responded to the emerging modern notions of property in order to consolidate their financial status even as they reinforced traditional boundaries in their private domain. This curious case reveals most dramatically a slice of the banker's life and of the city's public order caught in the throes of transition from one dispensation to another.[28]

The case began with an instance of theft that was detected around the second week of November 1800 when a bag of jewels together with other valuables and money went missing from the elaborately guarded premises of the banker.[29] The theft seems to have occurred following a family wedding. Suspicion fell on an old servant, Jairam, whom Arjunji had entrusted with the care of the jewels. The banker in accordance with local practice summoned a 'conjurer' to divine the thief. The conjurer came to a quick conclusion and accused Jairam, his brother Raghunath and his father-in-law Puniah of having committed the theft. A Brahmin retainer was immediately sent to Puniah's house to bring the accomplice to Trawadi's premises. There was a show of resistance when Janki Jagdip and Haribhai, two other brothers of the accused Puniah, went to the banker's residence demanding an explanation. Trawadi's principal, Bhucan, refused them admittance while Baru Jamadar, the banker's security guard, used physical force to turn them away. In fact Jamadar threatened them with violence and also hinted that they had better watch their ways as the guilt of the accused had already been established. Intimidated by his words the brothers left leaving the three suspects detained in Trawadi's premises. They were confined in different rooms, beaten up and ordered to confess. Jairam was kept in a dark room, possibly a storeroom or perhaps a cellar, while his brother and father-in-law had to make do in a privy. The confinement lasted for more than a fortnight, during the course of which they were allowed only bare essentials—parched gram and water, and visits to the toilet. They were periodically flogged by the security staff led by Bhucan and Shaikh Baru. The beatings got progressively worse, forcing the desperate Puniah to try to escape. On 8 December Puniah managed to stage a dramatic escape, the news of which provoked the banker to instruct his servants to use more force to extract a confession. What followed was a gruesome interrogation. About ten men seized Jairam, beat him with sticks and hides, and tied a sturdy rope fastened to a ceiling beam around his waist. A large grinding stone was placed on his back and the prisoner was left in this condition for the rest of the night. He cried repeatedly for water but it was not before dawn that he was given some relief. By this time his condition had deteriorated severely—at about six in the morning he was found foaming at the mouth and was slipping away. The staff tried to revive him with sips of water and ginger but to no avail.[30]

So far all that had happened in the wake of the robbery: the interception of the suspect, Jairam, and the punishment inflicted on him by his master who had regarded him as a son, had remained a private affair. His death altered the situation overnight as considerations of private entitlement and righteousness confronted the tenets of public justice. A number of uncomfortable questions cropped up—was the senior banker guilty of murder? Or was he a victim of circumstances over which he had lost control? Was the death of his servant intended and a consequence of intimidation or was it entirely accidental? These were tricky questions that the Company had to grapple with. It had just entered Surat as its ruler in 1800 and had appointed a magistrate to administer criminal cases. But it had neither the experience nor the confidence to take on the local banker who immediately invoked the strength of custom and scripture, and threatened withdrawal of support to the Company at a time when its position in the region was vulnerable. However, the Company for the moment had no option but to set its law in motion—Trawadi Arjunji Nathji was restrained under Section III Regulation III of the Act of 1800. Ramsey the judge stated quite categorically that he 'wished to avoid any degree of severity that may be improper as from the considerations of the advanced age, the peculiar status of a Brahman and also his extensive concerns as a shroff'.[31]

The trial that followed saw a slew of depositions—from the relatives of the deceased, his neighbours as well as from members of the banker's household and security staff. Discounting slight variations and garbled statements, the depositions agreed substantively on several counts: Trawadi had loved and cared for his servant and had treated him like a son; he had instructed his staff to extract a confession and was not aware of Jairam's deteriorating condition following the severe punishment that had been meted out to him. In other words his intentions had been clear—only to extract a confession and nothing more. But was this intention as innocent as it was made out to be? Did the banker not comprehend the severity of the interrogation? Was he in fact so oblivious to the prisoner's condition on the night of 9 December 1800? Also there was the trickier question of categorizing the incident as an act of private punishment inflicted by a Brahmin master especially as it entered the domain of the legal system the Company was trying to put in place. There were no easy answers given the fact that the trial occurred at the cusp of transition, and social and political realities could not be ignored. Trawadi Arjunji was both a

Brahmin notable whose influence was as yet not subordinate to the rule of law, as well as a banker who had bankrolled the Company's political projects. Neither of these factors could be overlooked.

The enormous influence that the senior banker commanded came into immediate and sharp relief, and by 13 December 1800, four days after the incident, a financial settlement bolstered by social coercion persuaded Jairam's relatives to withdraw the case. Trawadi's impassioned defence invoked the notion of caste values and credit reputation—both of which, he urged, were at risk in the trial. He maintained that he was not guilty, that he had no idea of Jairam's precarious condition and that he was incapable of harbouring malevolent intentions towards a person he had considered a son.[32] There were a few dissenting voices that suggested that the banker was not as innocent as he made out to be and also that the Company officials were aware of the robbery and detention and even implicitly supported the banker's actions. However, all this was hushed up and the verdict went in favour of the banker. The court in its concluding statement stated that 'from the circumstances that have been proved in the course of the trial, they cannot think that the prisoner ever intended to deprive Jairam Jugdees of life, but they are decidedly of opinion that the evidence they have heard has fully established that he was privy to the very illegal punishment inflicted on the dead which was the cause of his death and originated in the prisoner's (Trawadi's) orders'.[33] Some form of justice had to be therefore meted out and here the Company officials opted for traditional scriptural prescriptions suggested by a Hindu pundit who they had consulted in the city. These amounted to certain monetary payments and compensation that were seen as acts of penitence. This suited Trawadi Arjunji who had in fact used his leverage with the traditional social order to elicit a punishment that in no way altered his status or his sense of self-esteem; simultaneously he had deployed his personal connections with the Company to build up his case with conviction.[34]

In his business dealings as well as in controversies, the banker had demonstrated his ability to straddle the worlds of business, and caste and social status. Straddling the two domains had been made possible by the very dynamics of transition politics. The rationale for the Company's expansion in western India had been constituted around the principles of fair trade and safeguarding the interests of the fair trader, and with it the ancillary conditions of justice and an impersonal law that the Company courts enforced. But this relied on fragile foundations with the result that the new dispensation had to accommodate the dynamics of what was called the 'inner politics of the city'.[35] This was configured around traditional normative principles of the kind Trawadi Arjunji invoked. For the banker whose private engagement with religion, ritual and philanthropy was built into his self-description the reality of the political transition had not altered the ethical order in which his self and relationships were constituted. This is not to exonerate the banker from the charge of abuse of personal power which he had undoubtedly exercised in relation to his dependent, but to reflect on the process of negotiation in an emerging colonial context. Taking a cue from Thomas Timberg's study[36] on the Marwaris one could legitimately argue that complete control over dependents within the firm and household was an important facet of business enterprise and that Trawadi, when he claimed that he had loved his servant and enjoyed complete rights over him as a father would have over his son, was perhaps echoing the conventions he had been used to. It is very likely that an integral feature of his commercial practices involved complete control over his network of dependents and retainers and agents. At the same time the fact that he responded, like all good merchants, to the benefits of the colonial connection and retained his private practices to reinforce his self-image as a good upper-caste notable of the city, holds the key to his business success. Trust and reciprocity that have been identified as the keystone of efficient pre-modern enterprise were articulated in a context of caste hierarchy and social relationships that determined status and marketworthiness. These enjoyed an institutional apparatus when the Company dispensation promised merchants certain concrete benefits and arrangements that appeared rational and conducive to business expansion. For the Company, the banker had to be kept in good humour, and in 1800 there was no question of it interfering in any way in the traditional modes of redressal. On the other hand there was no question either of giving in to demands—even if symbolic—that threatened to question the Company's political profile. For instance in 1808 there is a petition from Trawadi's agent mentioning how his master had had a church built in Surat at great expense and that he was determined to affix an image there and that he wanted some guns fired from the Surat garrison at the time of consecrating the image. The authorities turned down this request saying that it was 'in every sense inadmissible as such indulgence was never extended by the government of which the flag still flies on the Castle and an acquiescence with it would be contemplated with horror and disgust by the most formidable part of the community'.[37]

From the fragmentary references of his later-day activities in the city of Surat it would appear that the banker continued to make endowments to religious establishments and built temples. One of these was the Balaji temple built at a cost of Rs 3 lakh which was subsequently endowed with the revenues of the village of Shewri that he had secured from the Gaekwad of Baroda. We do not know how long his firm remained solvent and what his successors did. But what is clear is how he became an integral part of the mythology constructed around businessmen in western India and how in this, the commitment to the Company, business, and ritual and religion was emphasized time and again. Little wonder then that later-day observers like Jeverilal Yajnik, talked of the enormous wealth of the banker, his steadfast loyalty to the 'Honourable Company' and of his lifelong deference to religion. Yajnik's letter also lamented the frittering away of Trawadi's affluence and the indigence of his descendants[38] during a period when Surat made way for Bombay and a new imperial dispensation dispossessed some groups and promoted others. What happened to Gujarati enterprise in the succeeding century and how fortunes were made and lost will form the subject of the next chapter dealing with the island city of Bombay and the exploits of its merchant magnates.

3. JAMSETJEE JEEJEEBHOY

THE FIRST PARSI BARONET

It might be thought that in this age, men were greedy of gain and so wrapped up in their selfish pursuits that they had no time to look after their neighbours or other things. But it was not so. Already David Sasoon had written his name on some of the greatest foundations of Bombay and Poona, benefactions comprehensive enough to embrace the crying wants of every caste and creed of our rapidly increasing population. Before 1848, Sir Jamsetjee Jeejeebhoy had gifted away £250,000 for the same noble purpose. There were men too who worked not only for themselves but for mankind and posterity venturing their lives and doing and daring everything to extend the boundaries of human knowledge.

—James Douglas, *Bombay and Western India:*
A Series of Stray Papers, 1893

THE LIFE AND career of Jamsetjee Jeejeebhoy (1783–1859) was inextricably woven into that of the island city of Bombay which by the time of his death had definitely emerged as India's great trading emporium and financial capital. Like the city which he made his own in very distinct ways, Jamsetjee began from modest beginnings to stake a claim on what was one of the most opulent of all traffic in the eastern seas in his time. His rise to pre-eminence in a real, foundational sense constituted one of the urban legends of colonial Bombay—a city that seemed to have enticed indigenous traders and businessmen to settle down and try their hands at business. It is true that Bombay's merchants and commercial residents had always enjoyed an easier—even if not entirely equal— relationship with their British mercantile partners and as a result participated in a more cosmopolitan and mixed society constituted by Hindu business communities, Muslim traders, and Parsi merchants, shipbuilders and entrepreneurs.[1] Jamsetjee Jeejeebhoy was an exemplary embodiment of Indo-European partnership as he rose to become one of the city's greatest merchants, philanthropists and public figures. What does this imply? Does it simply speak of an individual's sagacity and far-sightedness that enabled him to take the right business decisions? Does it speak of a particular moment in the history of global trade and business that his lifetime coincided with? Does it whisper about a very special moment in the history of a city and of a community? Does it gesture to a particular formation of capital and entrepreneurship that one has subsequently come to associate with the Parsi community? To a certain extent the answer would be an affirmative on all counts and yet such an endorsement would not do justice to the individual talent and temperament of a man whose ability to endure reverses, build networks of trust by refusing to compromise with personal integrity and reputation, see through calculated risks and revel in building a fortune, was indeed remarkable. Admittedly as a member of a community whose participation and experience in productive pursuits had always elicited notice, his values, assets and choices were in a sense prefigured. But what was striking and indeed unprecedented was the way he turned these to develop not just a stupendous business enterprise but a comprehensive engagement with ideas and institutions of modernity that catapulted him and his community into a larger global fraternity. It is this aspect of Jamsetjee's life and labour that set him apart from predecessors like Arjunji Nathji and enabled his contemporaries and successors to follow the trail that he had blazed. It was a case of engaging with the ethics of modernity, maybe even of what has recently come to be articulated as bourgeois dignity;[2] a commitment to an ideology of service, which saw profit and philanthropy work hand in hand to create and participate for the benefits of a modern public culture.

To write about Jamsetjee Jeejeebhoy and his exploits is not an easy task. Not because one is strapped for information but because there is an overblown mythology built around him by later acolytes and admirers who also happened to be publicists for the Parsi community—all engaged in putting together a coherent history for themselves and framing it within the narratives of industry, ingenuity and model minority behaviour. This is not to detract from the collective spirit of industry that the community seems to have enjoyed; early European observers tended to look at and represent them in flattering terms, initially as skilled craftsmen and artisans and thereafter as reliable clients and brokers.[3] What made the community especially receptive to enterprise has been a matter of speculation among scholars. The attempt here will be to focus on one merchant and on the heady business of making money and of what it took for this merchant to attain the heights of global capital from his base in Bombay and then to cultivate the virtues of a respectable bourgeois in the city's newly emerging public sphere. Two particular elements are essential to this story: first, the changing profile of Bombay as it slowly realigned itself to the emerging global economy of multilateral trade from the end of the eighteenth century; and second, the specific circumstances of the Parsi community in Bombay city whose location and functions in a nodal centre within a global network proved crucial.

The city of Bombay formed the nucleus of the English East India Company's settlements in western India from 1669. From the very beginning of its presence in Bombay, the Company authority's attempts to develop it as the principal mart of the region by holding out to local commercial society the positive advantages of protection, legal security, and even favourable custom duties did not meet with much success.[4] Migration of merchant groups from the more commercial regions of south Gujarat was sluggish and even those who did take up residence treated the new city as a place of temporary sojourn preferring to operate from Surat which remained, at least until the 1790s, the main financial and procurement centre for the region.[5] This was partly because the trade of the region continued to be oriented towards West Asia and directed from Surat, which Bombay could not offset for the greater part of the eighteenth century. The official trade of the Company from Bombay did not count for much and the private trade of its officials was conducted largely from Surat in collaboration with the city's favoured merchants. On the other hand Bombay was recognized as an important city of the future by the Company officials who made efforts to develop its infrastructure. The formation of a naval police to safeguard the seas from both the rival aspirations of local coastal chiefs as well as from piracy in the high seas meant that local merchants began to see the benefits of trading through the port of Bombay. Local merchant societies from Gujarat as well as the Konkan began to slowly accept the superior protection of the Company even while maintaining some degree of continuity with other channels of protection and adjudication. Protection came in the form of a pass or the licence to use English colours (flags), the possession of which, according to documents, safeguarded the bearer from the financial demands of other coastal chiefs and conferred the benefits of the Company's convoy. The value of such protection was not always apparent or even substantial, and merchants on several occasions found it to their advantage to exploit the porousness of maritime spaces and work through a multiple-pass system—accepting passes when necessary and jettisoning the practice whenever possible. However, by the middle of the eighteenth century the decisive victories of the Company's marine force over two important coastal contenders, especially along the Konkan littoral—the

Angrias of Kolaba and the Desais of Savantwadi[6]—persuaded local merchants to opt for Bombay as the chief outlet for local trade, and in the case of the Parsis held out immense possibilities for entering the city as service providers and shipwrights, given their expertise in artisanship. Parsis were well known for their artisanal and building skills; in fact Lowjee Nasserwanjee Wadia, a reputed carpenter in Surat, was persuaded to move to Bombay to help in the setting up of a dockyard. Lowjee's services enabled his family to receive important favours from the Company so much so that the position of Master Builder remained with them for more than three generations. Like other Parsi shipbuilders Lowjee was adept in copying and integrating European shipbuilding designs. This meant that the creation and expansion of the Company's naval force, the Bombay Marine, had extremely important implications for the Parsi community. They made their way into Bombay city in large numbers to offer their services in a variety of occupational capacities and to build close linkages with English power, and so emerged as a visible group in the city.[7]

It must also be kept in mind that the community primarily based in Gujarat (with their principal nucleus in Navsari) had always been disposed to the energetic pursuit of specialized occupations. Contemporary European travellers extolled their industry and work ethic. More recent work has suggested that the Parsis did not develop occupational specialization on the basis of religion, hierarchy or ideology. What is definitely apparent at least on the basis of available European observations of the seventeenth and eighteenth century was the level of skill and craftsmanship the community seems to have demonstrated in the fields of weaving and shipbuilding, and then translating these into a higher level of economic activity. From weavers to brokers to merchants and entrepreneurs the Parsis seem to have demonstrated all the great classical stages of capital accumulation and development that Marx had spoken of. Whether such a general assertion is tenable or not is beside the point—what is moot for consideration is how they responded to the opportunities that Bombay represented. Of course as has been recently demonstrated the Parsis have tended to view and envisage their history almost entirely through the optics of colonial experience and this may not be entirely reflective of a larger sociology of change and assimilation.[8] Yet on the basis of evidence it would seem that the community even in mid-eighteenth-century Surat began to gravitate towards the European trading companies—initially working for them as brokers and retail suppliers and then actively as their collaborators.[9] They migrated to Bombay in large numbers where they offered their services as local mediators, carpenters, victuallers and shipbuilders. Drawing from an existing network of commercial and retailing activities they were able to bring a depth to their new commercial activities in Bombay. They even bought property in the fortified area of the city and their numbers increased steadily through the course of the century. They were able to do this partly through fortunes they built up and partly through land estates they secured from the Company in return for the services they had provided. The family of Cowasji Rustamjee

Patel, for instance, received land in Thana and Bassein while the Wadia shipbuilders owned palatial estates in Mazgaon, Breach Candy and one called Lal Bagh in Parel. Cushioned thus by state support and individual initiative, it is little wonder the community should have been catapulted to wealth and status as the city's leading Shetias.

It was in such a city that Jeejeebhoy, born in 1783, was to found a fortune. His father who was a weaver died when Jamsetjee Jeejeebhoy was still very young but one does not know under what circumstances he moved to Bombay from Navsari. Presumably he was mobile and at the same time could draw on family and community networks, for, as an orphaned lad to be able to move to Bombay and take up residence with an uncle did suggest close familial connections.[10] His uncle who later became his father-in-law was a *batliwala* (a seller of bottles and presumably even of perfumes, for there are references to Parsis being in the fragrance business in Surat). His uncle, one may legitimately speculate, was one among the early Parsis to respond to the opportunities that the English city of Bombay seemed to offer. As a young person, presumably about thirteen or fourteen, Jamsetjee like the legendary Dick Whittington dared to dream, and more impressively, take the plunge. Equipped with some rudimentary language skills (Gujarati and a smattering of English) and bookkeeping techniques he took the momentous decision to try his luck in foreign trade. Evidently living in Bombay in the latter decades of the eighteenth century he was responsive to the sudden rush of energy that seemed to characterize the local commercial society poised on the brink of a take-off. This was a time when the lure of trade with China, sustained largely by a rising demand for raw cotton and thereafter opium, became a major temptation for the city's merchants. There were a number of advantages that local Indian merchants enjoyed in Bombay and its hinterland in Gujarat that made it possible for them to participate in this traffic alongside European merchants. These advantages were to do with better commercial intelligence of markets and produce, and of supply channels. The young Jamsetjee was not impervious to the prospects of trade as he imbibed the robust dynamism that Bombay as a trading space demonstrated. The city bustled with merchants of varying ethnic identities, with markets where an incredible array of goods was bought and sold— ranging from pearls to cochineal, cotton to dates.[11] The settlement also saw these merchants experimenting with not just business deals, but also negotiating new institutions like the Company's Mayor's Court and adjudication system, and building on friendships with foreign merchants. Growing up in such an atmosphere Jamsetjee's decision to wade in and embark on the new trade with China was not surprising even though it was certainly an act of daring and courage. But before tracking his first voyage, the trading world of the Indian Ocean and on the trade revolution that Bombay was on the brink of witnessing around this time, must be dwelled on.

Until the late 1780s Bombay remained a dreary settlement[12] resembling the backwaters that flowed into the city regularly. The city had been unable to take off as the great trading city

its founding fathers had envisaged, largely on account of
financial constraints the Company faced in this region which
made it impossible for it to develop an ambitious project.[13]
The Company in Bombay, unlike its counterpart in Bengal
after 1757, lacked an adequate territorial hinterland from
where they could count on regular revenues. Compounding
the geographical disadvantage, the constant pressure from
local competitors—especially the Marathas, the Company's
principal adversary—and the meteoric rise of Calcutta with
its growing trade with China (in what is called the great shift
to the East) meant that the island city had practically no
visibility to speak of. It remained a struggling settlement,
participating in a low level of commercial activity that
accommodated local merchants as well as overseas traders
from across West Asia, and was seen primarily as an extension
of the regional trading circuit with its centres in Surat and
other parts of coastal Gujarat. All this changed dramatically
around the 1780s when changes in global trade impacted the
western-Indian economy and enabled Bombay merchants to
expand their trading ventures. Until this time the city's
merchants—both European and Indian—had busied
themselves with the export and freight trade generally referred
to as the 'carrying' trade in the western-Indian Ocean as well
as in the coastal trade along the western Indian littoral. The
bulk of the trade was in raw cotton exports, rice and textiles
which continued to figure as an important item in the markets
of Hindustan. We have an interesting contemporary
document on handloom production and the deployment of
looms in Surat city during the 1790s which reflects quite

clearly, how even in this period, when Gujarati textile exports to West Asian markets were contracting, their consumption and distribution in the markets of upper India remained significant.[14]

The developments in the late 1780s and 1790s however, presaged a profound transformation for the city's merchants especially the Parsis who had already aligned themselves to the English power and had profitably entered the businesses of shipbuilding, shipping, respondentia and marine insurance which they conducted in partnership with the city's European merchants. The second half of the eighteenth century had seen a slow growth in the city's coastal trade as well as its connections with West Asia, East Africa, and Southeast Asia including China. Local merchants as well as Europeans and resident Arabs participated in this trade, drawing on old networks and connections and building new ones. Dates and pearls from West Asia continued to flood Bombay's markets while Chinese ceramic and silks found new buyers. Bombay thus became a fertile meeting place for Indian and Asian traders as well as European merchants. Bombay's coastal trade in grain, coconuts and textiles enhanced the cosmopolitan and local aspects of the city as a growing trade centre of the region. The growth of the respondentia business was the single-most distinguishing feature of Bombay's commerce in this period. The institution or practice of respondentia seems to have been fuelled by the rise of what is known as 'consignment trade'[15] which belonged especially to that domain of European private commerce that functioned outside the system of the Company's official business. A good idea of the respondentia business, its features and problems can be had from the disputes that came up for adjudication in the Mayor's Court at Bombay.

The essence of the consignment system, as Asiya Siddiqi suggests, was risk-sharing.[16] A venture would typically start with a shipper or a group of them consigning a cargo to an agent. The latter was entrusted with the charge of shipping it and selling it in a market. The shippers were backed by respondentia lenders and dealers who loaned money to them to get cargoes ready for the voyage. The agent to whom these goods were consigned normally paid an advance to the shipper equal to two-third of the estimated value of the goods which were considered the property of the shipper until they were sold and accounts adjusted to mutual satisfaction. The terms on which respondentia lenders came together were laid down in the form of an agreement wherein they contracted to give up their claims if the goods were lost due to an unforeseen accident. A shipowner or freighter presumably raised respondentia money at a higher rate of interest to compensate the lender, for there was a provision that expressly stipulated that no repayment be made if the voyage failed for some unforeseen reason.[17] Respondentia lenders in turn entered into detailed insurance arrangements as a security backup. Two features distinguished the expanding respondentia business in Bombay from the mid-eighteenth century: one was the growing collaboration between European private traders and Indian merchants in the city; and the other was an intensification of the integrated credit networks that supported this Indo-European business. Banias and Parsis were involved as brokers and respondentia lenders, insurance agents as well as shippers, while European traders functioned as agents for their associates back in England as well as being independent respondentia merchants. The arrangements did not always proceed smoothly—there were protracted disputes about the manner in which policies were read and construed, with the Mayor's Court of the Company endeavouring hard to reconcile local practice with the new legal procedures that it was seeking to put in place.[18]

The 1780s and 1790s saw a quickening of the city's commercial activity in which the European merchants began to assume a greater share. Not only were there more voyages to China, there were also important structural changes in European trade and business activity. With official prohibitions on private trading by the Company's servants the decision to break out on their own became pervasive. In most cases a young servant or the son of a London shipowner's family came to work in India and after a few years started to buy and sell commodities on his own account. If and when he met with success he registered a new business in partnership with a friend or two, and by pooling resources mounted trading operations.[19] It was from these beginnings that agency houses came into existence in the 1820s—the formation of which signified a new stage in Indian overseas trade. By the 1820s there were ten agency houses[20] in Madras, fifteen in Bombay and forty-six in Calcutta, which undertook the marketing of export goods and became involved in what could be called asset or wealth management. Their financial base was sustained and supported by the savings of depositors—mostly retired personnel of the Company—and they undertook the responsibility of marketing the goods that were shipped on their account. Merchants consigned their goods to the agency houses which provided an advance to them in anticipation of what the sales were expected to yield. Historians have argued that such a system of consignment exposed shippers to risk while leaving the agents virtually risk-free. Shippers had no way of questioning the price at which their cargoes were sold while agency houses were only too happy to operate on the capital of the shippers, blithely collecting their commission. They liked pure commission, for, as was so often remarked, 'income comes to you without asking, in the snug way of the China trade'.[21]

The emergence and ascendancy of agency houses in western India went through several identifiable stages. In the first phase the houses were primarily interested in cotton. From the latter decades of the eighteenth century the growing interest of private merchants and the early agency houses in cotton assumed political dimensions as they pressed the Bombay establishment of the Company to incorporate cotton-yielding territories into their sphere of influence.[22] Indigenous merchants in Bombay—both Parsis and Bania—participated in the traffic at different levels. Even as senior Parsi merchants of Bombay like Dady Nasserwanji consolidated their interests in shipping and the cotton trade, Bania merchants stepped forward in financing the trade in cotton with Gujarat, functioning as 'guarantee brokers'. From the 1770s the Parsis were already operating in the China trade, undertaking small ventures—their interest and investment undoubtedly emerging from their connections with European private traders, and consolidated impressively under Jamsetjee Jeejeebhoy. By the 1780s the trickle had turned into a flood as the increasing demand for tea in Britain and the interconnections among India, China and England, facilitated a hyper-profitable new triangular trading arrangement which was predicated on cotton, opium, tea and bills of exchange.[23]

The fillip to Britain's tea trade was provided by the famous Commutation Act of Pitt. The Act reduced duties in Britain on tea imports from China and improved the prospects of buying China's tea with exports of Indian raw cotton and opium. What this implied was that Indian export staples of cotton and opium could be bought and sent to China for tea. The connections and trade integration that followed rested on and expanded the existing networks of supply and retail trade in these commodities and which were for the most part operated by Indian merchants—some operating in collaboration with English private traders. At the same time the conditions of relative fluidity in the Indian Ocean that came in the wake of Anglo-French hostilities generated a new wave of merchant adventurism making it possible especially for Indian merchants in Bombay and other parts of western India to sail under different colours and with passes. Local merchants were persuaded to try their luck in the shipping and export trade that was directed from Bombay. Thus one finds references in the Mayor's Court registers to merchants from Kutch and Kathiawar sailing to Muscat and East Africa, and Parsis making voyages even further afield— some like Jamsetjee venturing as far as Britain!

Bombay's cotton trade with China began to show a perceptible growth from about the late 1780s. This was occasioned in part by crop failures in China and by the growing influence of European agency houses that sought to open up the trade to the East and find new markets for British manufacture. These two developments set the stage for consolidating Parsi interest in the export business to China. In fact one of the distinguishing features of Bombay's trade in the latter half of the eighteenth century was the cordiality and coexistence among Indian merchants including Parsis, Konkani Muslims and Hindus, and European mercantile firms[24] and the growing collaboration between the Bombay merchants and the agency houses. Indian shippers consigned goods to European agents and agency houses in addition to allocating some consignments of cotton and opium to Indian agents in China. The point that needs to be emphasized here is that China was increasingly seen as an important place to try one's luck, and several Parsi merchants in the city including Jamsetjee's uncle had started making short trips there by the end of the eighteenth century. It must also be mentioned that while raw cotton was the initial commodity that catapulted western India into global trade it was really opium that made Bombay's fortunes and those of its notable commercial men. The trade in opium also coincided with the second phase in the expansion of agency houses in India—the setting up of the partnership between the Parsi merchant Jamsetjee and the agency house of Jardine Matheson and Company.

Statistics on trade and shipping in Bombay tell a fascinating story of cotton-, opium- and Parsi-shipping that details both the interactions between the shippers and the agents who served the Company's interests, as well as the interaction among the shippers, agents and brokers (the two often the same) who undermined and flouted the Company's monopoly while supplying the magic drug through other channels. We will follow each of these skeins to appreciate how the extract of poppies entered the rivers and seas to supply the smoking dens in China and in the process enabled men to make millions and embark on voyages that surpassed their prior imagination. But first one must look at cotton and how this commodity positioned Bombay and its commercial society in the new colonial trading economy that was being assembled around this time—an economy dominated by the requirements of the Company and European private traders who were entering the eastern seas in increasing numbers, penetrating new markets and displacing some groups while collaborating with others.

From 1800 to 1813, of the 129 or so vessels registered under the port of Bombay, thirty-three carried raw cotton to China.[25] The reasons for this dramatic shift to the East were produced by a complex combination of local and global factors that had serious implications both for those who used the opportunity to capitalize on the demand and for those who were compelled to grow a cash crop over which they had little control. While famine conditions in the southern provinces of China forced farmers to take up grain cultivation in place of cotton, there was the pressing requirement for tea as a global export commodity. Reduced duties on tea had hugely increased demand for the commodity in England.

But the question of supporting its purchase remained. What this meant was that tea imports had to be supported by appropriate export items that would take off the pressure from Britain's bullion reserves. It was here that the newly acquired possessions of the Company in the Indian subcontinent came to assume central importance. For these were found to be ideally poised to play the required role in more ways than one. The Company's expansion especially into the cotton-rich tracts of Gujarat enabled intra-Asian trade or country trade to grow and serve the wider needs of British imperial finance and remittance—factors that became more important when opium came to dominate the three-way traffic. Essentially what cotton and opium did for British trade and finance was to make available desirable export staples with which to purchase tea. But this was not all. Its modalities made possible a multilateral and multidirectional traffic in remittances. A triangular trading relationship evolved that worked as follows: England imported huge quantities of tea from China; these were exchanged for the cotton and opium from India that was in demand in China. This in turn facilitated flows of remittance for both the English trading company as well as private merchants whose operations the Company had always encouraged. As early as 1773 it had been decided to float schemes to attract money from Bengal to Canton which could help the Company with tea purchases. The logic was that if bills on London at a reasonable rate of exchange were freely available, large sums of money would flow from English traders who would use this channel to remit funds back home. Thus an Englishman in Bengal wishing to send back his fortune could do so via Canton; he could for instance lend it to a shipper to buy cargoes for Canton. The implicit understanding in such a transaction was that on the sale of the cargo the proceeds would be offered to the Company's agents in Canton and who on their part would provide bills of exchange on London. This mode of multilateral remittances solved the needs both of the Company and of private traders intent on sending their profits home. It was this combination of circumstances and imperatives that led to the triangular trade structure that Tan Chung describes as 'Indian opium for the Chinese, Chinese tea for the Britons and British Raj for the Indians'.[26]

Historian Huw Bowan makes the important point that even before Bombay's rise to prominence, the export of cotton from Calcutta had set the basis for remittance operations which became more pronounced in the latter decades of the eighteenth century when private shipments captured the trade between India and China. Between 1774 and 1785, almost 60 per cent of all the cotton imported into China from British India came in privately owned ships. At first Bombay predominantly exported 'Surat cotton'— especially the fine, medium staple variety grown in Broach district—but cotton grown farther to the north of Gujarat began to rise to prominence during the 1790s. In 1787 the Bombay merchants reported that the 'Hong merchants of Canton confess that cotton from hence, even when they give what we deem is a high price, is much cheaper than their own, and that on trial is found to be of a quality fit for their every purpose.'[27] Soon Bombay cotton became one of the 'necessaries' of China as Lord Macartney observed on the occasion of his visit to China.

European private merchants along with Parsis dominated the intra-Asian cotton trade. Both groups worked in tandem and were able to bear sufficient pressure on the Company government to ensure its smooth operation. Agency houses like Forbes and Co. and Bruce Fawcett and Co., and Parsis like Dady Nasserwanjee and Framjee Cowasjee among many, emerged as principal exporters working with an extended supply chain that was dominated by up-country Bania merchants. The Parsis functioned in close collaboration with the agency houses and kept up a steady pressure on the Company authorities to safeguard the coastal channels so as to keep them free from piracy (mostly on cotton boats) and to facilitate smooth business transactions up-country where conditions of war and strife occasionally impeded supplies. These representations worked to a point but ultimately the traffic showed signs of decline, its vulnerability resulting from ineffective control over the supply channels. Local factors and cartels of supply merchants and dealers who were able to effectively bypass the system of control set up by the Company continued to manipulate, regulate and dominate supplies, to the detriment of the Company and European traders. Private merchants and the Company in Bombay were confronted by a range of local organizational and logistical problems related to raw cotton supplies and their difficulties were compounded by the fact that they knew very little about the market conditions in China. With opium the situation was different, not in terms of the trade's performance as far as remittance was concerned, but in working with relatively accurate market information on supply and demand. In fact it was in this department of commercial intelligence that Jamsetjee Jeejeebhoy was especially vigilant; both biographers and later-day historians have commented on his extraordinary attention to detail in the voluminous correspondence he maintained.

The shift to opium that cemented Bombay's breakthrough came during the first quarter of the nineteenth century and was made possible by the appearance of what was known as 'Malwa opium' and its growing presence in the city's export traffic to China. On paper this amounted to smuggling—a clandestine trade, as the Company endeavoured hard to enforce its monopoly over the production and distribution of opium in eastern India namely Bengal and Bihar.[28] In practice the Company had no option but to conform to the Chinese imperial edicts proscribing opium and turning over its distribution to private traders. But the competition posed by Malwa opium was nonetheless serious for it threatened to undercut prices. The very fact that Malwa opium was able to contest this monopoly and enable local merchant-speculators to make money and thereby accumulate capital is in itself a fascinating story but for the moment one must look at how this opium entered Bombay and into the calculations of the Parsi and European merchants of the city who undertook its transportation to China. The emergence of opium as the global commodity par excellence also embodied the second phase in the history of the agency houses when firms like Jardine Matheson came to the fore.

The origins of the firm of Jardine Matheson go back to 1787 with the arrival of Henry Cox in Canton who with his partners drove a lucrative trade in bills, Indian cotton and Bengal opium. By 1819 the firm was looked after by Charles Magniac who collaborated with James Matheson of Calcutta and William Jardine of Bombay to tap into the potentialities and possibilities of opium trade especially by investing in Malwa opium[29] which was not susceptible to the same official control of the Company unlike the Patna opium that was under the control of the Calcutta Council of the Company. Alain Le Pichon's analysis of the house of Jardine Matheson offers one important insights into the complex and interlocking operations of the Company, private traders, agency houses and the Parsi merchants of Bombay who were firmly entrenched in the city's China trade. What his analysis reveals is the extraordinary increase in the volume of tea consumed in Britain and in the volume of opium exports to China that were required to pay for the tea. Most of this trade was handled by private merchants—and given its illicit nature (the commodity was officially banned in China) the Company was quite content to sell the produce by auction in Calcutta and then live off its sales and proceeds. In Pichon's words, 'in reality it could not have survived financially without the proceeds from opium sales which the private trade invested in its bills'. While the Company was able to impose a monopoly in Bengal it could not do so in western India leaving private merchants—Indian and European—an even larger playing field for buying, selling and exporting the drug. This was the background for the rise and resurgence of the house of Jardine Matheson and its historic association with Jamsetjee Jeejeebhoy.[30]

In 1799 with the help of a comprehensive set of regulations the Company established a virtual monopoly over the opium business in eastern India. Known as the Bengal Regulation it sought to enforce tight controls over the production and cultivation of poppy. The peasants in Bengal and Bihar needed licenses for opium cultivation. These set out in detail the exact amount they could cultivate under their designated acreage. The entire crop was subsequently made over to the Company who processed the raw opium and packaged it in their factories before shipping it to Calcutta and thereafter to Canton where private traders and agency houses took charge of its sales. However, even before the Company could reap the benefits of their Bengal monopoly, disturbing reports began to circulate about Malwa opium being sent 'clandestinely' from the west coast. Notwithstanding the exaggerations that normally attended such rumours and biased reports it soon became evident that substantial opium consignments were making their way into China and were threatening to upset the Company's apple cart. Around 1800–1802 reports began to circulate that opium supplies from Bombay were increasing exponentially forcing the Company to declare an official ban on the Malwa produce. Like most bans this was badly enforced and did not work thanks to the predictable nexus among merchants, dealers and competing political claimants along the west coast, and also because all of Malwa opium was produced outside British-ruled territory in western and central India where the Company had little authority to meddle with production and distribution. The efforts that the Company undertook to persuade chiefs either to prevent the transit of Malwa opium through their territories along the coast or to restrict opium cultivation proved futile as they were hardly in a position to dislodge strongly embedded vested interests in the trade. Interested parties included revenue farmers, petty traders and dealers in opium, and the big bankers—referred to as sahukars—and wholesalers who bought up the stock in bulk. Stationed in commercial towns like Ujjain, Indore, Ratlam, Mandsaur and Pratapgarh, they worked with Parsis and the Bania merchants of Bombay and entered into regular arrangements with them. The latter in turn worked with and for European agency houses and private traders who were dependent for their opium purchases on the Marwari sahukars and Gujarati dealers.[31]

Thus by 1820 thanks to the increasing popularity of opium[32] as an export-cum-remittance commodity, and to the growing addiction of Chinese to the drug, opportunities for Indian merchants to participate in what was evidently a lucrative trade with China began to open up. In the case of Bombay and western India there was no question of the Company monopoly making a dent on the local trading network. The opium agency that the Company set up to regulate purchases by auction did not have teeth while the Company's attempts to persuade rulers in opium-producing areas to restrict cultivation were by and large ineffective. However, this is not to discount the importance of the new colonial trade in opium with China which had important implications for a variety of groups ranging from the British private trader to the Parsi shipper and the Gujarati/Marwari supplier and, most of all, to the peasant producer of the crop. Whole swathes of land were now under poppy cultivation and the fact that world prices and their volatility affected the small faceless cultivator underscored some of the more brutal aspects of early globalization. But equally the emerging situation generated unexpected opportunities for some merchant groups and enterprising individuals to take the plunge, calculate risks and embark upon enterprises that catapulted them to the position of global players in an international market. It is in this context that one can appreciate the exploits of Jamsetjee whose success was only partly an extension of his community's location in the island city and more significantly an expression of his personal energy and associations. Admittedly Parsis enjoyed a marked degree of proximity to the colonial power but even more significantly they had access to shipping, to older connections with private European merchants trading in opium in China and were able to exploit Bombay's access to a larger opium-producing hinterland in central India and Rajasthan.

There were several kinds of opium transactions in Bombay.[33] Firstly, there were big purchasers in Bombay who bought some of the opium on their account to be consigned to agents in China. Among these agents were the big European houses like Magniac and Jardine Matheson, and there were Indian agents in Canton. Some of these agents were long-standing and had been working for more than two decades in the wake of early Indo-European ventures in China and Southeast Asia. Hirji Jivanji and his brother Maneckji were among the first Parsis to go to China and establish business contacts.[34] The Jivanjis owned several ships, many of which were for the China trade. The Jivanjis' China trade proved profitable, bringing the family into ready money—a surname they adopted (Readymoney). Like so many other Parsis they too translated commercial wealth into charitable largesse for the Parsi and other Indian communities. Secondly, there were petty traders at auctions who, as Farooqi mentions, usually bought the opium for immediate sale to actual exporters. These men were generally small investors who made use of the price fluctuations from one auction to the next to make quick profits. Thirdly, there were purchases made at places on the coast, like the Portuguese enclave of Daman, by big and small Bombay merchants who were able to enter and direct a clandestine trade in the produce.[35] As Amar Farooqi has mentioned in his work, Bombay along with Daman further north along the littoral, virtually constituted a unified market as far as Malwa opium policy was concerned. By 1829 the Company government in Bombay abandoned their Malwa opium policy, convinced that it was no longer possible to continue with it given the rampant increase in smuggling. This decision had important consequences for private merchants.

It is evident that to the young and enterprising Jamsetjee the world of Bombay's trade smacked of adventure and possibilities as he saw merchants big and small, Indian and European, speculating and sending cargoes. Family connections helped as his cousin, Merwanjee Manekjee, allowed him to act as apprentice and even sent him on a voyage to China in 1799. We do not have any information on this trip but one can presume that he was deeply impressed with the flurry and excitement that characterized the China trade.[36] It is also likely that in Canton he familiarized himself with the agency business, having decided to enter the consignment trade in a small way. Jamsetjee's marriage to Awabi Framjee on 1 March 1803 made his forays to China possible as his father-in-law, Framjee Pestonjee—a Bombay merchant and a small but significant player in the China trade—enlisted him as a partner in his trade and organized four more trips in quick succession. The fourth voyage saw destiny playing its inscrutable hand, testing young Jamsetjee's endurance and patience even as it brought him in contact with an Englishman, an association with whom would transform his life forever.[37]

It was the year 1804 when destiny stepped in. At this point of time the Napoleonic Wars were in full throttle and their echoes resonated strongly in the Indian Ocean as well. The antagonism and rivalry between England and France assumed a global dimension. The dynamics of the Anglo-French hostility exposed ships sailing under their respective colours to attack and capture on the high seas, an experience that the young Jamsetjee was about to encounter. Equally there were possibilities for adventure as merchants could exploit the ambiguity of jurisdiction on the high seas to their advantage. In July 1805 nearly four months before the decisive Battle of Trafalgar, the Company's ship *Brunswick* was captured by the French off Point de Galle. Jamsetjee found himself in company with Willam Jardine (who had risen to the station of Assistant Surgeon in the service of the Company) both of whom along with a crew of Asiatic passengers were transferred to a ship to reach the neutral Dutch station off the Cape of Good Hope.[38] The two men got to know each other more intimately when the ship met with a gale and was wrecked off the Cape. Thankfully no lives were lost and it was during this calamity that the two men bonded and entered into a friendship that not only survived the ravages of time but also became a positive basis for an unprecedented business adventure.[39] Fortune, it is said, favours the brave, and at that moment of crisis no one could doubt the fortitude of the two men or indeed doubt the thirst for enterprise that characterized both the Scot and his Parsi counterpart. Both men had the strength of established networks behind them; both were familiar with the carrying trade to China and both had assiduously cultivated contacts in Canton, Calcutta, Madras and Bombay. By this time Jamesetjee had already established a network of contacts in the East—in China, Colombo, Penang, Sumatra—and it was only a matter of time before he would expand the small business that he operated with his uncle and set up a lucrative partnership with Jardine and his associates.

From this time Jeejeebhoy's career as a successful merchant developed rapidly. The first decades of his career until about the 1830s were heady days for the trader. Aware of the enormous potential for profit in the opium trade with China, Jamsetjee developed two kinds of business strategies. One was to maintain a diverse portfolio that included shipping, export trade and remittance business, and the other was to work at strengthening and expanding his network of contacts, both on the marketing side as well as supply chain. What was so remarkable about Jamsetjee was his ability to read market trends and demonstrate accurate judgement when it came to choosing his contacts. It was this almost uncanny sense that won him admirers and lifelong friends including the Portuguese merchant Roger De Faria. His associates were drawn from diverse backgrounds.[40] Between 1805 and 1817 Jamsetjee seems to have invested wisely in developing a fleet of ships of modest tonnage—between 500 and 1200 tons—which he acquired and built mostly along the west coast and then turned over to the transportation of opium. He consigned his cargo to the agency houses especially to Jardine Matheson and Company that emerged as the largest in terms of operations in Canton. His personal connections stood him in good stead as he secured favourable prices. On the other end of the spectrum his association with Marwari sahukars who were involved in the opium business, particularly in its supply from central India to Bombay, meant that he was in a position to comprehend and control the supply channels of the trade. Thus one finds Jamsetjee buying both at the Company auction and, through his access to Malwa opium, in the alternative markets that fed into the Daman route and which the Company failed to control; thereafter the produce would be sent to China, consigning it to agency houses.[41] He worked with Magniac and Company, sending them cargoes and regularly taking care to ensure the quality of the consignment. He traded on his own account as well, sending substantial quantities that brought in impressive returns. He does not seem to have participated in either the commission business or guarantee brokerage, both of which he is said to have abhorred, but it is not clear whether this was part of the later mythology that was built around him. Besides focusing on the Bombay–China market Jamsetjee also exported a substantial quantity of opium and cotton from Calcutta, and cotton from Madras to China. His affairs at Calcutta were handled by Jardine Skinner and Company in which Jardine's brother John was a partner. Jamsetjee was part of this network and not only did he benefit from the circuit of information and trust, he also offered advice to facilitate mutual business. By the 1820s Jamsetjee had already built up a huge fortune—according to contemporaries, to the tune of Rs 2 crore—and by which time he had invested in substantial properties in Bombay.

The strategic framework of Jamsetjee's China operations was the consignment trade that worked in tandem with agency houses who assumed responsibility for marketing the exports despatched.[42] Jamsetjee as consignor or as agent acting for other consignors financed the cargo, and as shipper was responsible for the management of the voyage. His trusted associates were members of agency houses who organized the sale at the other end. While the resident agent was compensated through commission on sales, the shippers claimed a share in the profits as a reward for their service. Jamsetjee's various consignors were largely European agency houses but included individual Marwari and Jain merchants as well. Jamsetjee thus undertook the purchase of opium, consigned and shipped it to agency houses in Canton, Macao and Hong Kong to sell them at favourable prices. The risk of sending the goods was his as consignor and so were the profits that accrued on sale. This meant that he had to be sure of the quality of the export item as well as its supply and price, and this involved an astute understanding of the supply market. He had to be equally confident about his associates in China whose intercession could help maintain a high level of profits given the attendant risks of the operations. It was here that personal connections and friendships mattered so fundamentally—in fact there were occasions when Jamsetjee took exception to the carelessness of agents in disposing of produce at favourable prices and allowing competitors to get the better of a deal.

A sense of Jamsetjee's astute trading personality and punctilious habits can be best had from the correspondence he maintained with his associates both in Bombay and Canton as well as in up-country central India. The letters are fascinating as they reflect his growth and maturing into a scrupulous businessman who showed an extraordinary energy and commitment to running his global business with an untiring attention to detail. The letters also capture some of the hectic and heady excitement associated with trade and the linkages between profit, philanthropy and social projects that Jamsetjee undertook in his later years. Between 1826 and 1849 Jamsetjee steadily grew in stature making his mark as an extraordinarily successful trader and a remarkable philanthropist, learning to cope with pressures that came from both government and other traders, including his China associates and consolidating his reputation as a responsible

subject whose wealth was channelled to social projects and
civic improvements.

Operating the opium trade was by no means an easy
business. Given that ships were still sailing into the wind and
opium was still being transported along muddy tracks or
along the coast via small boats, it was not easy either to
predict markets or ensure supplies at competitive prices.
There was also the question of ensuring at all times the
cooperation of agents in China and of negotiating with the
government when it attempted to introduce new licence
fees. And yet amidst all these pressures it was Jamsetjee's
steely resolve to drive a bargain and maintain transparency
with his associates that made his partnership so valuable and
ensured the kind of success he enjoyed, almost first among
equals. His letters give one a lucid sense of his ability to speak
tough. Thus by 1849 he was able, quite explicitly, to write to
his associate Jardine about the acute sense of disappointment
he felt at the Englishman's opium transactions. He wrote:

> I will candidly confess to you that my silence of late has
> been occasioned by a feeling of dissatisfaction at your
> transactions in opium on our account. Day after day I
> have felt a disinclination to enter upon a correspondence,
> the style of which is so different from what we have
> hitherto enjoyed and while I believe that it may prove
> disagreeable to you, I can assure you that it is not the
> less so to myself.[43]

That he was able to write with such authority was a
consequence of years of trading experience and diligence. He
was untiring in his efforts to keep abreast of market

developments and prices, not to speak of resisting any attempts by the government to tax the trade. Equally he was able to exert sufficient pressure on the government over issues of safeguarding the quality of the export product. His advantages lay in his network of contacts and in his intimate knowledge of the product and process of opium cultivation that allowed him to time his purchases at the best prices and ensure quality supply. Writing to Magniac and Company on 25 May 1831 he spoke about how the stock of Malwa opium that season was less than anticipated and also how on close examination the stocks in Daman were found to be inferior and were consequently rejected. He also referred to high prices of the product which he observed could be attributed to 'the very scanty' supplies because 'at the commencement of the cultivation of the poppy, which took place in November last the prices for the drug were exceedingly low in Malwa whereas for grain they are in the very reverse and this alone was sufficient to induce many of the ryots to turn their attention to the most profitable commodity and the consequence was that a great deal of land previously devoted to cultivation of poppy was sown with grain.'[44] However, Jamsetjee insisted that the following years' crops would be more reliable and 'under all these circumstances, we cannot divest ourselves of the hope that your market will yield remunerative prices, and although we do not in the slightest degree wish to influence or bias your mind, what we would recommend are unbending firmness on your part which has always had the desired effect on the Chinese.'[45] Here was a hard-nosed businessman at work who was forecasting and assessing his risks and advising on market decisions so that the business could yield what was commensurate with the investment.[46] Friends and relatives were integral to his business network—not only did they handle important aspects of the business but they also ensured and safeguarded the circulation of information so vital to the export trade. On 20 February 1830 he wrote to William Jardine about how he was taking care to buy the right quantities of cotton, sugar and opium, and what he considered safe speculation and what he did not. He also wrote to James Matheson informing him of how wisely his friend Motichand was chartering a French ship to take opium which would be disposed of on the most advantageous terms. On another occasion, on 12 December 1845, in a letter to Matheson he referred to his efforts in acquiring a very superior product and that he was hopeful of getting an excellent price: 'I regret I could not procure more and you can expect very little of this kind in future, therefore you better not part without making the Chinese pay handsome prices, otherwise hold little longer.'[47]

Jamsetjee's letters and reports reveal forcefully his deep engagement with the business that he operated in conditions of risk and uncertainty. The need of the hour was to keep a close and vigilant watch on prices and supplies and to ensure that his agents exerted themselves to secure the best prices. The difficulties of ensuring these conditions come out vividly in the letters as does the integrity and solidity of the network. Regular communication with his agents in China revealed how familiar the merchant was about local difficulties and the loopholes in government policy. A letter to Magniac and

Company dated 17 March 1829 is revealing and replete with details. It referred to the Company's sales, how the competition among buyers—mostly the Macao Portuguese and local merchants—was the chief cause for pushing up prices of the narcotic at the point of purchase, and how caution had to be constantly exercised in pursuing this business.[48] This was especially emphasized in a letter dated 20 April 1829 which referred to improving opium prices but also advised caution on not making too many purchases of Malwa opium. At the same time the letter detailed the many interruptions that opium transportation in central India faced. The discord and rivalry among chieftains in the region disrupted supplies and rival chiefs 'prevented camels from going beyond a certain place; as soon as agents heard the news they forwarded proper persons to arrange with both powers (i.e. the rival parties concerned) and secure protection.'[49] Because of the interruptions and the additional costs of protection prices of Malwa opium were high, forcing Jamsetjee to exercise the utmost caution in his affairs. The regard and respect that he maintained for his friends and associates constituted the real basis for his business and it is evident that it was his sense of personal integrity and commitment that enabled him to survive several uncertainties and difficulties in his operations. The 1840s on the other hand reveal an irritated Jamsetjee as he faced losses on his opium account for which he held his associates responsible. His letters to Jardine in 1849 reveal his annoyance at the indifference that he and his associates demonstrated in executing Jamsetjee's business. As he put it:

That the opium trade I know little better than many people do, respecting the market and consumption and having transacted a long series of years in this drug speculation. Care must be taken in purchasing largely when cheap and not to buy when dear but you sanguine too much upon China friends. You must have received China news by this mail we are prepared to sustain heavy losses; you did not use good judgement with caution—you have received several communications from me but you pay little attention.[50]

In fact the 1840s were trying times for Jamsetjee as he faced serious challenges in his opium and remittance business. From very early on, the close intersection of the trade in bills with that of the opium trade meant that the house of Jamsetjee was extensively involved in the business of remittance. Here too, ties with British associates proved crucial. As noted on a previous occasion remittances were built into the structure of the China trade as all parties involved expected or were required to send back proceeds from one point to another besides ensuring funds for purchases in Canton. Merchants needed to send sales proceeds back home. The Company required funds to buy tea consignments in China and so was happy to give bills on its treasury in London or in India. Finally both European merchants and the Company needed to remit their proceeds back to England. At every stage the parties concerned were on the lookout for bills, both private and the Company's. Jamsetjee found bills on the Court of Directors convenient as these were in great demand among European traders in India who wished to make remittances home. In July 1826 he sold bills on the court amounting to 20,000 pounds sterling.[51] He had his own agents in London who discounted bills issued on which Jamsetjee earned handsome commissions. Clearly, the poor son of a Navsari weaver had arrived as he took his place among the most intrepid of merchant adventurers sailing to the East. Little wonder then that his name became synonymous with Parsi enterprise and acumen. His letters are replete with his concerns in procuring favourable exchange rates and/or silver consignments; on 16 December 1849 he wrote to Jardine mentioning how there were no purchasers for bills and that there was still left undrawn a large fund in London.[52] Despite these difficulties he was able to hold his own and not only pass down a valuable business to his son but also enter into an active public programme of philanthropy.

The difficulties that bedevilled Jamsetjee's business were largely connected to the changes in the structure of the China trade following the end of the Company's monopoly over it in 1834. This happened to coincide with major shifts in shipping technology that began to displace sail with steam and which gave Europeans an even more decisive advantage. It is in this context that historians have concluded that Jamsetjee despite his extraordinary success was unable to fully subvert the asymmetry that the colonial power introduced in the business scenario.[53] Once the Company's monopoly on the China trade was abolished, a critical channel in his business network—the agent in need of funds and bills—dried up. Bills on the Company were also becoming less readily available; to get around this Jamsetjee resorted to several expedients. On the one hand he urged his agents at Canton to send ingots of Chinese silver in payments; on the other he began exporting Chinese tea and silk on his own account to London. Occasionally he also sold bills of his firm to residents in Calcutta and Bombay which could be discounted by his agents in London against the funds received from the firm of Jardine Matheson. He also tried to reroute his funds from China to India via Britain by importing British goods—textiles, iron bars and copper—into India. None of these proved satisfactory especially as the end of the monopoly saw big British and American firms enter the market, whose influence in the interlocking arrangements was ever greater thanks to the larger credit reserves they operated with.

Even as the astute businessman was juggling his options, changes in maritime technology presented a fresh set of difficulties in the realm of shipping, a sector that had catapulted him into the world of global trade in the first place. Steam ships began to enter the scene around 1840 and Jamsetjee's country craft proved to be no match for these new vessels whose considerably lower running expenses gave them enormous competitive advantages. For instance he was amazed to find that free traders could sail their ships to England at a much lower cost; three or four pounds sterling per ton while he could barely sail his own for less than seven or even nine pounds sterling. At the same time he found ships becoming difficult to maintain. The competition that small ships faced was not easy to contend with and as he wrote in a letter to his friend:

> We have now in Bombay harbour an immense fleet of
> free traders who are willing to take on cotton to China
> for the very lowest freights, at which it is impossible to
> sail a country ship. Last year, many of our fine teak
> ships were laid up, and this season would have gone at
> miserably low freight.[54]

He complained that people were not coming forward to give
them freight—'they were afraid to come to us'.[55] His son met
with the same difficulties and while persisting with his father's
business confessed that the presence of free traders and
Yankees had made it impossible for them to compete.

With a serious crisis brewing Jamsetjee decided to cut
short his losses by selling his ships. This coincided with acts
of arson on country shipping as a number of ships owned by
British and Indians (including those of Jamsetjee) were
burnt.[56] Whether this act of arson was motivated by labour
agitation or by anti-British sentiment is difficult to establish
with complete certitude. However, the fires certainly created
a panic among shipowners and merchants, and in the long
run the British authorities linked these fires with their ongoing
efforts to undercut the customary Indian system of labour
recruitment. Jamsetjee on his part would appear to have
given up his interests in shipping. He then concentrated his
efforts on trading on his account, on lending to shippers and
on investments in insurance, railway companies and joint
stock banks. What is striking about his business activities is
the ease with which he stepped into the modern domain of
business, very much like the house of Tagores in Calcutta,
but with the important difference that he was able to deflect

commercial crises better than his Bengali counterparts. It is evident from both contemporary and retrospective accounts that his prestige never flagged. He invested in real estate, bought valuable properties, maintained an active public life and showed an extraordinary commitment to the notion of public good. Here it would appear that his own humble beginnings had convinced him about the need for looking after the lesser endowed and for giving the less privileged a leg-up.

What was especially remarkable about the manner in which Jamsetjee conducted a business whose scale was impressive by any standards was the close surveillance he exercised over the market and the attention he paid to keeping his network intact. Going by his voluminous correspondence it is evident that he had his ear close to the ground and he was able to anticipate market behaviour by appreciating the several variables at work. These included speculative enterprise carried on by local business groups like the Marwaris with the volume of business they conducted along parallel networks which ultimately impacted the opium traffic he and his agents carried on.[57] Equally important was the way in which he was able to use his influence in the city both to persuade the government to withdraw any undue measure that added to the costs of trade and also to get a fair dealing for his smaller associates when their investments were jeopardized by the Opium Wars. He relied on his friends in England to press claims for indemnification arguing that many of the local merchants were vulnerable and likely to lose considerably. For him trade and business operations constituted a way of life and it behoved on all parties concerned to play it by the given rules. As he mentioned on a number of occasions it was not just a question of speculation or of spending time but a serious activity that was built on calculation and judgement, and one that relied on integrity, and commitment to standards.

Jamsetjee did not take long to decide how he wished to spend his great fortune. As a contemporary journal commented, 'The responsibilities and the duties which cannot be separated from wealth, but which Christianity itself is often powerless to enforce upon those who profess it, were a portion of his natural religion.'[58] In 1822 the first public act of his philanthropy came into view as he released several prisoners confined in Bombay jails—for debt—under the authority of the Small Causes Court. To do this he spent a sum of Rs 3000—no small amount. It is interesting that he should have picked this issue as a public cause for it indicated his concern with both the idea of credit and how it had to be socially supported and also his interest in looking after small merchants who in all probability had run into debt because of funeral- and wedding-related expenses. As the correspondent for the *North American Review* observed:

> A man will frequently spend on these occasions the prospective earnings of years, which usurious moneylenders stand ready to advance at exorbitant rates of interest. The poor debtor, pressed hard and cheated, often falls into a state of inextricable difficulty; his little possessions are seized by his creditor, and he himself is cast into jail and ruined. It affords an indication of the

smallness of the sums for which individuals are often confined, than with this amount of three thousand rupees.[59]

Jamsetjee satisfied the claims of more than fifty creditors—an act that certainly gestured to a very exceptional public spiritedness. We have no details regarding the social composition of the debtors and whether or not they were exclusively members of his community.

Jamsetjee's acts of charity[60] were as visible as were his business ventures. These ranged from donations to hospitals, educational activities and urban improvements, and went beyond serving the interests of his own community which he did through the Parsi Panchayat. To what extent did these represent an extension of traditional modes of giving? After all both Parsis and non-Parsi mercantile groups were accustomed to making acts of benefaction. Did Jamsetjee's philanthropy represent a shift in values, gesturing to an altogether new concept of public responsibilities? The historical record of merchants making donations and sustaining endowments confirms the impression that for Hindu communities, acts of munificence were primarily directed to propitiating deities and reinforcing the idea of individual status and honour. When it came to Parsis it would appear that by the end of the eighteenth century acts of giving tended to become institutionalized and were narrowed down to the community itself. In the case of Jamsetjee, the decision to embark on serious philanthropy both for his community and for the larger collective good may be seen to have been an offshoot of his engagement with notions of modernity acquired through his trading connections and business associations with Europeans. In relation to the suggestion that such acts of philanthropy could have been efforts at gaining social capital instead it may well be argued that his participation in an expansive public culture was part of his engagement with a new cosmopolitan modernity that Bombay's social fabric supported. This was evident in the interest he showed in developing schemes that were aimed at the welfare of the larger population in Bombay and Surat and in dedicating some of his charity work to the memory of his close friends like Motichand Amichand. The Bombay government was struck by this expansive temperament. Speaking on the occasion of the negotiations leading to the establishment of the Hindoo Benevolent Fund the government observed: 'The scheme proposes a peculiar feature of liberality in contemplating the benefit of a class of the community different from that to which the donor belongs.'[61] Equally striking was his pursuit of a model for institutionalizing philanthropic activity almost as a business concern in order to arrive at a system that ensured the security of the principal sum or deposit.

Much of Jamsetjee's efforts were directed at improving the social sector in Bombay city.[62] This involved investment in real estate and the setting up of important endowments that would look after social and educational needs of the city's population. That the island city was seen by the first quarter of the nineteenth century as a ramshackle cosmopolitan space which beckoned individuals to try their luck was evident to both locals and foreigners. It was reckoned the least traditional and the most cosmopolitan of all eastern cities, representing a patchwork where 'Brahmin and Buddhist, Mussulman and Parsi, Jew and Christian jostled each other at every turn.'[63] The city provided, even if inadequately, access to private and public spaces—where business could be pursued, justice availed in the existing courts, claims on urban space legally contested, and family or private traditions followed in the privacy of one's home. The negotiation of public space for community concerns was not smooth but in that process of engagement a new and urgent sense of the 'public' was fostered.[64] Parsis were especially vigilant about this. There are numerous allusions to how their life had a 'half-eastern and half-western character. At the counting houses and their shops, they appear like merchants and shopkeepers in the West. But their life at home, in their private houses, is quite after Eastern fashion. Their wives and other females, though less secluded than is common among Hindus and Mussulmans, are kept much out of sight, and hold a low and subordinate place in the household.'[65] The receptivity of the community to western influences even before western education was institutionalized would explain why Jamsetjee too was able to take a stand on public matters and opt for institutions and practices that made him a genuinely modern person. His interventions embodied the moment when the community broke out from its commercial mould. That they were self-conscious in their choice of the colonial patron was no secret. Consider how Menant observed: 'The evolution which has turned an exclusively mercantile caste into the one priding itself most on its education and its intellectual pursuits was only beginning to develop'[66] by the mid-nineteenth century, and soon the Parsi was no more the broker of the Europeans but one who sat next to him on the benches of the corporations and donned the robes of an English gentleman. Jeejeebhoy played a major role in this transformation as he initiated schemes for the upliftment of his community, intervened in the affairs of the Parsi Panchayat and also undertook larger schemes for the public good that made him Bombay's most distinguished son.

One must first look at the various acts of philanthropy that Jamsetjee undertook. Besides providing financial assistance to destitute families and debtors in distress, he undertook an extensive programme of public buildings to serve his community in the form of improvements and modifications to cemeteries and sacred buildings, as also to house the blind in Navsari. He also made generous subscriptions to the Parsi Panchayat. These acts were evidently an expression of his commitment and concern for the community but were also intended to enhance his personal status within it. The Parsi Panchayat whose function was to frame rules for the regulation of the community's affairs dated to the early eighteenth century. From the very beginning it was dominated by men of influence and by the end of the eighteenth century, became a site for contestation. Not only was there the spectacle of notables fighting for its control, the body did not enjoy legal authority to enforce its decrees relating to marriage, inheritance and conjugality, and eventually as the Panchayat became utterly discredited the community had no option but to turn to English law.[67] This as it happened was a double-edged sword—for while on the one hand it gave disaffected Parsis an alternative forum to ventilate their grievances, it also underscored the community's marginality and vulnerability. It is likely, as some historians have argued, that the senior members of the community began to entertain social aspirations of reclaiming a more standardized narrative of tradition for the community instead of vacating the space for the colonial authorities, European scholars and missionaries to write their history. For instance in 1844–45 a series of letters from Manekjee Kharshedjee appeared in the *Bombay Times* where he exposed the misdemeanours of some members of the Parsi Panchayat that had lost all credibility by then. By 1855 the *Bombay Times* noted that the Panchayat's power hung on a mere thread of public opinion and could 'be sundered by a newspaper's paragraph or a barrister's brief'. For the colonial state all this revealed the utter hollowness of a primitive tribunal that had no option but to make way before the 'advance of civilization'.[68]

Understandably under the circumstances influential Shetias like Hirjee Readymoney and Jamsetjee Jeejeebhoy realized the threat posed to their community's profile and mobilized support for overhauling laws and setting a more substantive basis from which to regulate its affairs. Such an orientation inevitably brought urgency to public welfare activities, intended by and large to enhancing the Parsi community's moral and material resources which would give back the community a measure of self-confidence and public visibility. Thus from 1842, after his knighthood, the old trader directed his attention to education and the creation of benevolent institutions and dispensaries to safeguard the interests of the marginal and disempowered.[69] He gave over Rs 30,000 to a wide variety of public and private causes: he provided famine relief, financed public works, and founded hospitals, schools, and scholarship funds. His best-known foundations were the Jamsetjee Jeejeebhoy Hospital and the Jamsetjee Jeejeebhoy School of Art. What made these interventions especially impressive was the interest he displayed in running these and in providing a substantive organisational basis to social welfare activities. It was here that Jamsetjee revealed a disposition that was managerially modern and which looked at social service as more than a mere extension of charity and largesse. All his ventures required the assistance of government whom he approached to act as executor of property and funds that were consigned to the running of charity. The idea was to deposit a certain principal sum in the government treasury at a stipulated rate of interest which would be allotted to certain specified agents running certain charities. This measure in his view was the only way that misappropriation of trust property could be prevented. As he wrote to his friend Charles Forbes in London urging him to use his influence with the Court of Directors to endorse his scheme of a Hindu charity fund:

> I have seen among natives so much mismanagement not to mention misappropriation of trust property leading to endless disputes as well as causing ruin among families. I am sure it will be deemed a great boon if government would consent to take charge from all parties willing to avail themselves of their agency of

property (that is Company paper) and pay interest accruing thereon periodically to persons named to receive it, government taking care that the principal amount should not pass out of their hands.[70]

The self-conscious and confident stand that Jamsetjee assumed in his charity schemes reflect above all the stature that he had gained in Bombay by the late 1840s. Reacting somewhat bitterly to the Court of Directors' initial reluctance to his schemes and to an additional proposed donation he wrote how he wished he 'could properly convey to the Court of Directors an idea of the increase which has taken place of late in the pauper population of the island and the wretched consequences'.[71] There were destitute members of his community who needed assistance and he wished more people would come forth with assistance as is evident from the following statement: 'I firmly believe that were it not for the daily charity exercised by a few natives towards numbers of those poor unfortunate creatures much sickness would prevail. I cannot but feel that they (the Court of Directors) have been somewhat wanting in that liberality of feeling which is their moral characteristic in respect to these little trifling matters. I have not been wanting in my services to the state. This I tell you my friend not in the way of a boast but only to show you that I have a little claim on the consideration of the authorities.'[72]

Like his business ventures that relied so critically on the support and goodwill of English associates and friends Jamsetjee was able to work with the same network in his social schemes. What stands out in his transactions is the commitment to a cause that was expansive and embracing, and also his sheer dogged advocacy of the same through official and unofficial networks of contacts. For him it was evidently not just a matter of making a splash or even enhancing his position within the community but to emerge as a prominent member of Bombay's changing population where he could demonstrate his organizational skills and share his vision of a modern city that cared for its subjects. He appears to have supervised even small details and one finds interesting references to ex-servants of the Company approaching him for positions in the new institutions that he set up. We have Mackie, a former surgeon with the Company, asking him for a job in the Jamsetjee Jeejeebhoy Hospital. In reply to this request Jamsetjee wrote quite candidly that while he was more than happy to have Mackie serving the institution he was not entirely sure that the government or Court of Directors (who were part of the hospital establishment as executors of the trust) would endorse his application. As he put it, 'You are quite aware of the prejudice that exists here against all those who are not in the immediate service of the Company and how frequently that feeling of prejudice operates to their exclusion from many privileges and emoluments even when they may be possessed of greater zeal and talents for the execution of their duties than the more favoured servants of the Company.'[73]

The attention and sustained advocacy of social causes and the increasing donations that Jamsetjee continued with despite difficulties could not but make an appreciable impact on the minds of the colonial administration. It earned him universal approval so much so that the Court of Directors recommended his name for the Queen's Honours List. Thus in May 1842 at an elaborate ceremony of presentation at Parel, the residence of the Governor, Jamsetjee was knighted. The address accompanying the ceremony spoke of the exertions he had made during crises and calamities in Surat and how his bounty and generosity had helped widows and orphans, the unfortunate and the destitute. It went on to say:

> ... neither is it necessary to dwell upon the benefits which the trade of this port has derived from the enterprise and magnitude of your commercial operations; nor to point out the great extent to which you have availed yourself of the means of doing good derived from your mercantile knowledge and experience, joined to a conciliatory disposition and the probity of your character, as well as from your position in the native community, by arranging differences and settling disputes, so as to save the parties from the evils of a tedious and expensive litigation.[74]

Lord Elphinstone went a step further when he rhetorically asked: which other world city could boast of 'a citizen who has devoted a quarter of a million sterling to purposes of public charity and benevolence?'[75] He also drew attention to the catholic character of Jamsetjee's benevolence—his sympathy for the poor and suffering of all creeds.

These were not just words of praise. They embodied in a very real sense the intentions of the colonial state to rationalize commercial practices in order to facilitate business in which project agents like Jamsetjee played a critical role. This is not to say that Jeejeebhoy was simply a lackey of the British and was happy to play the role of a comprador but to make the larger point that he was in his orientation and enterprise willing to endorse the larger capitalist project that could be ensured by rational business practice that undergirded the colonial trading economy. This involved among other things a new mode of resolution and the institution of more formal safeguards for property and one that theoretically at least avoided needless litigation, working as it would on principles of personal integrity, reciprocity and a public espousal of the law. However, it must be observed that his embrace of British rule and capitalism was not selective and that over time he became, as so many other Parsis did, genuinely committed to the project of modernity with all its accoutrements of associational politics and education. Furthermore unlike his later-day counterparts for whom the business of safeguarding identity became more urgent, he demonstrated an openness that was perhaps symptomatic of an age and a location that was not as paranoid of the western encounter. Admittedly Bombay's location and the specificities of western India's historical experience made it possible for local business groups to operate at a time when colonial forces produced serious distortions elsewhere. Indeed even in western India, as Jeejeebhoy found to his consternation, the business of shipping and remittance was not easy to navigate after the 1830s but what saved the day was his ability to diversify his portfolio and systematize business practices and networks which he was able to transfer easily to his son and successor.

Jamsetjee Jeejeebhoy died on 14 April 1859 and was

succeeded in the baronetcy by his eldest son, Cursetjee Jamsetjee, who in 1860 assumed the name of his father. What had distinguished Jamsetjee's business career was his unequivocal commitment to a personal-cum-business network that was vital to the betterment of his own business. There were no considerations of morality or ethics about the trade in narcotics, the poison drug that was being exported and which constituted the base of his enormous wealth. The idea was to drive a lucrative trade which demanded association with the British free traders and agency houses and also with local suppliers and wholesale dealers. It can be argued that he went out of his way to serve Jardine Matheson and Company but then it must also be kept in mind that the latter's business principles emphasizing attention to detail and transparency of information as well as prohibition of speculation on individual accounts were valuable business lessons that Jamsetjee learned. Little wonder then that he entertained the agency house so consistently and endorsed its dealings at every step. The *Bombay Courier* on 4 June 1842 carried the following item—one that summed up the essence of the relationship that proved so vital for the personal fortune of Jamsetjee as well as for the trade of the community and the city.

Friends and constituents of James Matheson held a meeting at Sir Jamsetjee Jeejeebhoy's house within Bombay Fort where Bomanjee Hormusjee read the following address to Matheson during his brief visit:

Whether we regard him in a commercial or philanthropic light, he merits our esteem and admiration. It is upon such characters that our commercial greatness is based. His liberality and munificence first originated the epithet "merchant prince". We wish him a full recovery of his health and happiness in his native land.

You have been a firm friend of the merchants of Bombay through dangerous and difficult times. It is nearly three years since the regular trade at Canton was disrupted. Your firmness, skill and perseverance has maintained our imports and exports. When £2 million was withdrawn from Indian capital by the surrender of the opium to Elliot we were paralysed until you generously provided advances for both the relief of your constituents in India and for us to carry on our China trade under foreign flags, which you arranged at your own great risk and responsibility. We could not ourselves have conceived of such a plan and our ships would have remained outside with their cotton cargoes rotting and with them our fortunes.

We want you to know how much we admire your judgement and determination. To remember your Bombay friends we have asked Magniac Jardine & Co. to present you on arrival in England with a valuable service of plate.

Matheson replied:

My services were nothing more than what a commercial agent should do for his constituents. That you consider them worthy of distinction reveals your own kindness and generosity. It was your liberal confidence in our firm when things did not always go perfectly that strengthened our hand as Agents. From our long experience of your style we were able to act as we did when Capt Elliot suspended British trade in 1839. I think you have over-rated the value of those services—we simply did for you what we would have done for ourselves. As the emergency was extraordinary, we adopted extraordinary remedies.[76]

These expressions of mutual appreciation colour contemporary correspondence and reportage and indicate all too clearly, the collective decision of the Parsi community and its principal merchants to piggyback on the British free trader to earn their place under the sun and in the process to engage with modernity. It would be too cynical to see in Jamsetjee's personal associations exclusively self-aggrandizing motives, and yet it would be unhistorical to overlook this and see the collective enterprise of Jardine and Jamsetjee as purely a matter of an extended friendship. What is apparent is how persuaded Jamsetjee and his Parsi friends were about the rhetoric of the benign consequences of free trade and how in this they actually perceived substantial advantages to follow. To this needs to be added the personal eccentricities of men who lived amidst heady days of fortune-making and were subject to all kinds of impulses that ranged from hard-headed business decisions to incredibly generous donations. We come across a number of interesting descriptions from contemporary newspapers about the righteousness and competence of private merchants like Matheson and Jardine who endorsed the Company of cheering free traders and who saw in their adventure a salve for the whole world. Note for instance how William Jardine on the occasion of his farewell dinner observed, 'I have lived here long. Our lives and property are better protected here in China than many other places in the World. A foreigner can sleep with his windows open without fear, guarded by a watchful and excellent police. Business is conducted easily and usually with singular good faith. The infrequent exception proves the rule. The courtesy of the Chinese in their business with foreigners is remarkable. These are the reasons why so many of us keep coming back and stay so long.'[77] He systematically refuted the idea of his community being smugglers. The Canton Register of 15 March 1842 was also unequivocal in its appreciation of Jardine Matheson whose efficiency and perseverance were singularly responsible for the success of British trade.[78] Both men made extensive references to the operations of Parsi merchants whose operations they viewed as perfectly legitimate vis-à-vis the hypocrisy of the Chinese government and the monopoly of the Hong merchants.

We need not simply look at public demonstrations of free traders' rhetoric and bonhomie as an exercise in excess. The Parsi embrace of modern trade and colonial modernity was a creative response and Jamsetjee played a pioneering role in this process of adaptation. The sheer audacity with which he dared to dream and the rigour and perseverance with which he drove his business, directing his attention to the most trivial of all details is what makes his life such an interesting story. The ways in which he located himself in the city and its emerging public life invested his endeavour with a dimension that set the standard for his successors to follow.

There was never in his case any anxiety about the ambiguity of trading in narcotics and being part of the opium regime. As far as he was concerned his attention was directed to good business values and market behaviour that saw China as the source of demand and India as the source of supply. It was a lucrative enterprise that had to be promoted vigorously and efficiently. Similarly there was never any question of contesting the connection with the colonial power—Jamsetjee viewed the partnership with William Jardine and other associates as part of an expanded patron–client relationship which was more equal than most and as a critical element in the success of his own enterprise. This is not to say that Jamsetjee did not experience the limits of the partnership or that he was unaware of the Indian losses during the Opium Wars that were not taken seriously by the British authorities, but to merely make the point that he saw the English connection as indispensable for his trading pursuits and, by extension, for his social projects.

4. PREMCHAND ROYCHAND

A MAN FOR ALL SEASONS

The possessor of an 'Open Sesame' which might have been envied by the romantic Ali Baba of Arabian Nights Tales . . . he was one Chemiagar (master alchemist) who could turn dust into the yellow metal, the one unrivalled magician who could by his magic wand transmute the sands of Backbay into solid nuggets of gold wherewith to pave the way to paradise.

—Dinesh Eduljee Wacha on Premchand Roychand, quoted in Sharada Dwivedi, *Premchand Roychand (1831–1906): His Life and Times*, Mumbai, 2006.

If Premchand had a friend to oblige, who wanted money, he recommended him for a loan. If Premchand had shares to sell, he would suggest to an acquaintance that he should buy, offering at the same time to 'finance' the purchase money by procuring him a loan from the Bank of Bombay. If Premchand wanted money for speculation, he would suggest to some friend to join him in it, and then procure a loan in his friend's name for the money required. His influence was felt not only at the Head Office, but at the branches also, the agents at Kalbadevi, Broach

and Surat all receiving instructions to consult Premchand or his
agents respecting advances.
—(Great Britain, Report of the Commissioners
appointed to inquire into the failure of the Bank of
Bombay

HOW DOES ONE reconcile these two observations? Was
Premchand Roychand a smooth conman who created the
illusion of profit to tempt his naïve prospectors? Or was he a
genuine speculator who had his finger on the pulse of the
market and was propelled by the romance associated with
commerce? Was he merely an opportunistic manipulator of
stocks, shares and schemes, or someone who also instinctively
knew how to create, consolidate and deploy networks of
association and information to his advantage? What moved
his imagination and gave him the necessary resources—
mental and moral—to ride through crests of success and
troughs of failure during the years that have been characterized
as 'an insane interlude' in the annals of nineteenth-century
Bombay? It is not easy to answer these questions. For one,
one is handicapped by the absence of first-hand information
on Premchand. There are only later representations of him
and his career by biographers and a fairly critical indictment
of his methods by an inquiry commission that was set up to
investigate the failure of the Old Bank of Bombay which he
had been part of. Reading these conflicting representations it
would seem that at one level he was the Harshad Mehta of
his times as he bought shares heavily at a premium across
many segments that included banks and land-reclamation

companies. He dominated the Bank of Bombay by using his personal connections and persuaded its directors and board to advance and sanction loans without proper guarantees. At another level there seems to have been something magical, even if illusory, about the way he was able to create a bubble and then survive its explosion and show true grit as he resurfaced and went on to build a substantial business for a second time, and thereafter assume public and civic responsibilities as a modern subject fashioned by colonial rule and its accoutrements.

To unravel the story of the complex life and times of Premchand Roychand is not easy. His biographers,[1] whether Dinshaw Wacha or more recently Sharada Dwivedi, tend to focus on the expansive temperament and grit of the young and almost entirely self-tutored businessman who looked for an opportunity and having found it, put it to good use. On the other hand economic historians of modern India like Dwijendra Tripathi and Amiya Bagchi have offered a more critical explanation of Premchand Roychand's business methods which were helped and endorsed by lax banking practices of British officials and directors in charge of the Old Bank of Bombay.[2] The latter used Premchand as a fence to drive and expand their own speculative ventures. Some contemporary British accounts tended to see him as the sole instigator of corrupt and venal practices who hyped the share mania in Bombay city while others suggested that European businessmen and interested bank officials were as much to blame for the disaster that followed the speculation bubble.

The truth may have been somewhere in between for

Premchand was simply too clever to have been used by the Europeans, and being fully aware of the loopholes in the banking system as it operated then, he was able to promote and push through speculative ventures in a manner that was unprecedented.[3] Evidently for him the business of making money and the excitement attached to it was an operative factor which impelled him to take risks that were fuelled by a volatile international environment and sustained by a supportive network of personal contacts with officials in power. Subsequently however, it involved a series of poor decisions and bad judgements especially when it came to appointing mediocre men in charge of new shell companies that Premchand sponsored. Senseless speculation was followed by a crash-and-collapse phenomena, but what distinguished Premchand from many of his other colleagues was his ability to rise again and not only make a fortune but also introspect about his personal actions and then discharge his larger responsibilities as a public person. It is in the interplay of profit and philanthropy, speculation and service that Premchand Roychand's life assumes a particular poignancy as it embodies the complexities of the colonial situation and the range of responses it generated among the local subjects of Bombay.

Like so many other merchants of the time Premchand Roychand[4] came from a Surati family of Oswal Jains—traditionally associated with brokerage, banking and retail trade. The community specialized in inland trade and brokerage and commanded complex and specialized business skills and commercial practices; moreover thanks to endogamous matrimonial arrangements it could draw on a network of reliable agents and partners. This aspect of Bania organization accounted for the resilience of the community and the ability to make the most of emerging opportunities, continually strengthen networks and take up residence in new centres with relative ease. This was historically true— from the days of the seventeenth-century Jain trader Banarsidas (author of *Ardhakathanak*) to Premchand Roychand's days the community was known to be excessively mobile, relying on carefully cultivated networks of familial and business contacts so as to expand its business operations and respond to whatever opportunities that came its way. It was the ability to mobilize, establish and deploy connections that explains why the Indian business and banking communities especially the Banias in Gujarat were able to survive regime changes and expand the scale of operations, keeping in step with the times and finding for itself a dominant niche within the overall business structure. We know for instance that by the latter decades of the eighteenth century substantial sections of the region's Bania population had migrated to Bombay from various commercial centres in western India, consolidating community linkages in the city— relying on traditional community practices and resources even as they maintained and improved their older contacts with the commercial centres in the larger region that could be put to use when the situation arose. This of course was vital when it came to a business like brokerage in cotton that grew in Gujarat and which had to be brought to the island city at regular intervals and made ready for the export markets.

At the same time the community, like its counterparts—the Bhatias and the Lohanas—was fully responsive to the new institutions that the city of Bombay represented, and could make full use of them, like the Mayor's Court for redressing grievances and for evolving a common understanding of commercial practices, bridging traditional norms with the newly emerging ones put forward by European private merchants and the English East India Company. Thus Bombay city developed very specific community-based residential quarters like Kalbadevi–Bhuleshwar where Hindu immigrants from Kutch, Kathiawar and Marwar settled down and made use of the new institutions and networks that the city offered. D.E. Wacha's reminiscences offer an excellent snapshot of the residential patterns in Bombay city. While the buildings in the northern part of the Fort area in Bombay belonged to wealthy Parsi merchants (the *shetia log* as they were known), the north-eastern part was the residential area of the Banias including famous bankers such as Atmaram Bhucan and Narottam Madhavdas. It was here that an army of *mehta*s, or clerks squatted every day in tiny shops poring over their account books engaged in buying and selling hundreds of bills of exchange.[5]

It is in this context that one needs to place the decision of Premchand's father, Deepchand Roychand, to migrate to Bombay. He was a mid-level timber merchant who in all probability had connections with Bombay's Parsi traders and dealers in wood, and decided sometime in the 1840s to try his luck in the island city. Legend has it that he brought his family—a wife, two sons and three daughters to the city of dreams on a bullock cart. The family took up residence in a small tenement at Champa gully in Kalbadevi–Bhuleshwar where the senior Roychand familiarized himself with business prospects; he enrolled his sons in schools that were part of the Bombay Education Society set up for the tutoring of local inhabitants.[6] We do not have too many details about Deepchand's early initiatives in Bombay but it would seem likely that he sensed where the opportunities lay and what sort of training and apprenticeship his sons should be given. His timing was not inappropriate—the city was in fact buzzing with expectations after a late and languid start in the greater part of the eighteenth century when its trade lay in doldrums. By the time Deepchand had moved into the city the situation had changed dramatically, largely in the aftermath of the opium trade and the growth in brokerage and banking associated with export trade.

What must have struck Deepchand or any other observer for that matter was the growing expansion of the opium and cotton trade with China and the resultant opportunities that were present for local businessmen working in various joint ventures with Europeans. It was soon apparent that associations with the city's European traders and officials were the way to go in order to penetrate the trading and financial structure of colonial Bombay. As mentioned in the context of Jamsetjee Jeejeebhoy's career Bombay had come into its own in the export traffic of India, attracting considerable local investment in the cotton and opium agency business. Jamsetjee's career, as indeed of other merchants'—both Parsi and non-Parsi—had revealed the benefit of European associations. Under the circumstances the senior Roychand seems to have lost no time in developing close personal contacts with Europeans and giving his sons the rudiments of an English education.

The city of Bombay by this time had already experimented tentatively with new educational institutions partly sponsored by the administration and partly by local subjects The Elphinstone Native Education Institution was one such instance which had grown out of earlier efforts like the Bombay Education Society. Here Indians could for the first time receive a systematic education in the literature, languages, science and philosophy of Europe. Prior efforts had registered a warm response—mostly from Parsis—not so much from Gujaratis whose engagement with education was initially lukewarm.[7] However, Deepchand had no doubts about the social and commercial potential of western education and the English language as an important medium of communication, and he persuaded his sons to opt for the same. The gamble paid off; not only did Premchand acquire a command over the usage of English, he was also able to put this to good use in developing close contacts with the city's European business community and the Bombay officialdom whose extensive involvement in trade became an important constituent in his future plans.

By the late 1840s the senior Roychand had already identified two lines of business for his sons—the cotton agency system and guarantee brokerage, and the banking business in Bombay. The city of Bombay, unlike its counterparts Madras and Calcutta, accommodated substantial Indian participation in its commercial and financial sectors, enabling Indian merchants like Roychand to enter the upper echelons of banking and brokerage. This was largely a consequence of the way that Bombay's trade and commerce had evolved between the 1840s and 1860s which was to have important consequences for industrialization in the long run. In the short run however, what Indo-European ventures in trade and brokerage[8] produced was the speculation frenzy in which Premchand played a key role. In either case the propensity for risk-taking and planning for the future on the part of the city's indigenous men-of-capital was impressive giving the island city a lead and ensuring its financial primacy well into the century and thereafter. For early official chroniclers of Bombay city the Indo-European speculation of the 1860s was also the key to Bombay's development as a modern city. With the cotton boom bringing in a colossal amount of capital, city expansion and infrastructural improvement followed, even as speculation turned to land reclamation and investment in real estate.[9]

The 1850s and 1860s saw a steady expansion of trade and an explosion of banking activity in Bombay.[10] What was especially important about this development was its implication for Indian merchants. Bombay's trade was primarily driven by the demand for cotton in China and England and subsequently in the home market as well which ensured a corresponding growth in the business of guarantee brokerage. Besides, the fact that historically in Bombay, private European and Indian capital was strong and had always bailed out the weak Bombay government meant that Indian merchants were able to retain a significant share in the city's trade and financial sectors. The Parsi community was especially visible in the export trade and manufacture while Gujarati business communities and Marwaris participated in guarantee brokerage before turning their attention to the emerging trade in stocks and shares. Anglo-Indian banking based in Bombay enjoyed greater Indian participation than other colonial cities.[11] Responding to these developments the senior Roychand seems to have quickly moved into the brokerage business and worked for several European partners whose favours he put to good use in subsequent years. Rising rapidly as a trusted broker and guarantor he built up an impressive network of associations including the directors of the Bank of Bombay whose investment interests, in the opinion of later-day critics, obscured better judgement.[12]

The cotton trade was the fulcrum around which Bombay's prosperity began to turn right from the closing decades of the eighteenth century. As the principal port for exports and given its proximity to the cotton-growing region of Gujarat and Kathiawar, Bombay and its European merchants had from the 1780s relied on substantial brokers to handle the trade in cotton. The Bombay merchants and agency houses used the brokers, whose operations were indispensable, in order to invest in substantial purchases, the financing of which was also undertaken by the local shroffs and their financial instruments or hundis as they were known. Studies have shown how the entire trade in cotton was founded upon credit and bills advanced to Bombay merchants by local financiers. Local organizational and logistical problems

associated with the supply and trade of raw cotton made the
dependence on Indian brokers and bankers inevitable.[13] These
were largely related to the limited control the English enjoyed
in the cotton-producing areas as well as the difficulties of
transacting with local currencies in Gujarat. The cotton
exported from Bombay was grown in the northward regions
primarily Gujarat and Kathiawar where conditions of political
insecurity often interrupted supply. There was also a chronic
problem of enforcing quality control which the cotton dealers
combined to resist. But the most serious factor was the
financial one. Cotton had to be purchased in local currency
or in bills, and it was here that the local Bania shroffs emerged
as vital links in the commodity chain connecting production
centres to collection points and finally to the port city.

In the late eighteenth century the hundi was seen as
indispensable for cotton trade as the Bombay silver rupee did
not circulate at par with the other local currencies in Gujarat
where purchases had to be made. The Bombay merchant
had neither the requisite cash reserves to finance purchases
nor the necessary familiarity with exchange rates that operated
between the Bombay rupee and other local currencies. Under
the circumstances city merchants by and large preferred to
work through the connections of the Bania broker who
could provide him with bills for a fixed sum to facilitate local
purchases. The shroff issuing the hundi was familiar with
two things: one, how much the Bombay currency would
fetch in Surat or elsewhere in Gujarat which in fact constituted
the real difference in the value of the two currencies; and
two, the additional charges that such a transaction entailed.

Consequently bills became major instruments in the purchase and procurement of cotton; the hundi network expanded, the ramifications of which became larger as trade and traffic grew in scale.[14] Bombay developed a vibrant banking sector and before the formal establishment of the Bank of Bombay, local sarrafs dominated the money scene, with their hundis servicing a huge range of operations—export as well as inland trade. The Bazaar Gate area was one of the principal headquarters for the banking business, with firms such as that of Motishaw, Kaka Parekh and Bansilal Abirchand enjoying enormous credit and goodwill.[15]

Banking or rather western-style banking in early nineteenth-century Bombay developed as an integral part of the activities of European private merchants and agency houses. The success of agency houses such as Forbes and Company, Fawcett and Company or for that matter Jardine Matheson and Jamsetjee Jeejeebhoy demonstrated the importance and potential of the export trade and commission business and encouraged the formation of business organizations such as the Bombay Chamber of Commerce and the Bank of Bombay by Europeans, as also the formation of commercial firms and enterprises by Indians.[16] In fact it was the concrete and formal articulation of Indian commercial initiative that set the Bombay experience apart. As mentioned previously Indians were active here—forming associations and investing in insurance companies and banking. Many of them owned substantial shares in enterprises such as the Bombay Insurance Society (1849–55) and the Apollo Cotton Press Company to name a few.[17]

Banks and financial companies were increasingly drawn to the export of cotton. This in turn reactivated the inland trade in cotton, encouraging traders big and small to emerge as guarantee brokers and assume agency for the cotton traffic. As early as the latter decades of the eighteenth century European merchants had relied on local dealers and retail traders stationed in the cotton-producing areas of south Gujarat and Kathiawar whose control over information of the supply chain and credit ensured their importance under the emerging colonial dispensation. Thereafter when cotton and opium exports catapulted Bombay to new and commanding heights, these suppliers remained important and their networks enabled later-day entrants like Premchand and his father to make good use of their community contacts to enter into cotton speculation decisively. The Bombay merchants—Indians as well as Europeans—were united in their efforts to bolster the trade as far as possible. Even as early as 1845 public debates about keeping the trade free from unnecessary impositions were rife. The *Bombay Courier* periodically carried important letters and comments on the cotton trade addressed by cotton merchants like Jamsetjee Jeejeebhoy and Ramdas Harichand among others.[18]

The practice of cotton speculation by Indian merchants in Bombay was a logical sequel to the business of guarantee brokerage that Banias and Marwaris had traditionally participated in. European traders and importers appointed guarantee brokers who were remunerated with a 1 per cent commission on sales and whose function was to guarantee the trustworthiness of other businessmen who dealt with the firm. The business of guarantee brokerage in the 1850s was shared by Parsis and Banias. Cowasjee Jehangir[19] for instance amassed a huge wealth as the guarantee broker of Cardwell Parsons and Company, while Premchand's father became guarantee broker to the Bank of Bombay which was floated in the 1830s. Deepchand Roychand in all probability sensed the lucrative possibilities of brokerage in cotton and in the hundi business which the local Banias had customarily been dealing in. Familiarity with the credit and remittance business encouraged them to enter the world of modern banking and stocks and shares. Premchand was thus quick to find work in 1852 with a senior broker in Bombay, Ramchand Lala, whose business he managed with considerable efficiency.[20] His ability to enter into connections with European merchants and bank managers stood him in good stead so much so that he became a full-fledged broker himself, intervening decisively in the business of guarantee brokerage—even buying up Lala's business. The Roychands now commenced trading on their own account. They bought and sold hundis and shares of the banks of the day. By 1858 they had amassed a fortune of one lakh rupees[21] and felt confident enough to take part in serious speculation especially as international developments propelled Bombay to ride the wave of the cotton boom. By this time the family had also invested in real estate—on 15 January 1855 Roychand Deepchand bought his first property in Kalbadevi[22] for a sum of Rs 2500 and the stage was set for the setting up of the firm of Premchand Roychand.[23] It is likely that the firm invested in jewels as well which became a form of security for some of the loans they applied for.

The expansion of the cotton trade and the consequent speculation surrounding it was an instance that demonstrated the extent of India's integration into the global economy in the mid-nineteenth century. It was a direct fallout of the American Civil War that severely disrupted US cotton supplies to England, forcing the latter to consider the option of Indian cotton which had not attracted much attention until then. However, in view of the changing circumstances it became necessary to find substitutes for American cotton in order to maintain the British textile industry. India was a natural choice given the availability of raw material and it was up to the establishment to try and push for expanded cotton cultivation and yoke it to the export market. The decision paid off as Indian cotton exports entered the market and its prices skyrocketed. Predictably brokers tasted profits and were persuaded to extend their investment. The figures below reflect the enormous expansion that Bombay's trade registered between 1861 and 1865.

Year	Imports in Crore (Rs)	Exports in Crore (Rs)
1861–62	10.19	26.34
1863–64	14.27	38.08
1864–65	14.46	40.52
1865–66	13.96	35.74

Source: Raymond Sullivan, *One Hundred Years of Bombay*, Bombay, 1937.

This early success held a foretaste of things to come. Impressive gains were made in brokerage as also by insurance companies and banks that were set up in Bombay driven by private enterprise. Even before the cotton-splash capital was moving into the new banks and insurance companies that were set up under European initiative. Some brokers achieved official recognition; it is documented that between 1840 and 1850 around six to seven Indian brokers dealing in bullion, exchange, stocks and shares (in banks and financial companies) were recognized by the Bombay government and European banks. These brokers were not formally organized but a group of around twenty-two who began trading under a banyan tree opposite the Bombay Town Hall contributing a rupee each to form themselves into an institution that came to be known as the Native Share and Stockbrokers Association which was eventually formalized as the Bombay Stock Exchange in 1875.[24] This development definitely indicated the coming of a modern western-type capitalism which was being adopted by the bazaar merchants. It was in such a milieu that the senior Roychand and his son operated in, in the 1850s and decided to vigorously participate in the trade in brokerage and speculation, using it to their commercial advantage to the optimum level. Both men correctly estimated that winning the confidence of European associates and directors who were investing in cotton and other shares in related companies was the need of the hour. Hence they stepped forward to work as brokers for English officials and European traders and thereafter the officers associated with the Bank of Bombay. From this point onwards speculation in cotton and later in real estate and reclamation schemes became one as far as Premchand Roychand was concerned. It was left for him to exploit the situation and to take steps to dominate the market and mesmerize it into submission.

What constituted Premchand's assets at this point of time? How did he assume a position of such control in the business of brokerage and subsequently of the share market? Was it propelled by local networking and official connections? Was it a result of greater attention to detail?—for, in less than seven years of joining the brokerage business, Premchand assumed a position of total control, with other brokers serving as associates and working in accordance with his instructions on how and when to invest. As Wacha, his biographer notes, Premchand's educational background, his courteous and charming disposition, his deep insight and quick calculation, and the advice he gave fructified into such happy results that he captivated the imagination of one and all. In Wacha's words, he 'was worshipped as such not only by his own fraternity but by the vulgar mass who floated like geese and willingly chose to be guided by him'.[25] Merchants in the city could not but be responsive to the immense possibilities cotton speculation held out in the wake of the American Civil War that had banks and brokers, financial institutions and companies scurrying around for speculation. The timing was of course perfect, for as the prices of Indian cotton skyrocketed so did the aspiration level of local businessmen, and it was easy to persuade them to invest in the crop and along with it in a whole series of allied derivatives. As Wacha put it, 'King Cotton was the great deity at whose shrine, between 1862 and 1865, the merchant and the trader, the rich and the poor, high and low, master and servant all paid pooja.'[26] It was a rare intersection when imperial interests and local speculation converged and set the stage for an unprecedented episode in the history of Bombay and indigenous capital. *The Bombay Gazette* in its issue dated 11 January 1862 carried a piece from the *Friend of India* that conveyed the excitement of the bazaar:

> The effect of the war was not visible in Liverpool till the beginning of the year and did not make itself felt till the end of March. Then did the government as well as the public realise the fact that a trade worth 50 million [rupees] [was] going [for] a begging and that India might have it if she were equal to the crisis. No experienced man ever entertained a doubt that India could fully meet the difficulty if only the concessions were made, a steadily high price and means of transit from the interior to the seaboard. The one was in inverse ratio to the other. The more roads the less price would be required to tempt cotton buyers—the fewer roads the greater price must Lancashire offer. Unfortunately the railway system was incomplete and the very districts that produced most cotton were those through which fewest roads passed. Then prices rose. The Bombay houses went wild with speculation. England said to India—give us a million bales this year and we shall be content.[27]

This was a dramatic turnaround from the previous years. In general Indian cotton was of the short-staple variety and had been seen as unfit for British mills. Thus until the late 1850s the tonnage arriving at the Bombay port was modest—figures reckoning this at 404,000. However, in five years' time this changed as figures for trade values were up to Rs 12.53 crore which included the value of merchandise and treasure imported and exported, which amount was Rs 8.42 crore in the preceding decade.[28] The balance of trade changed dramatically once the British government aggressively encouraged the substitution of American cotton by Indian supplies.[29] From this point onwards the demand for cotton grew at an unprecedented rate as government and private initiative encouraged cultivators and dealers to trade in the commodity. Moneylenders and bankers hurried to enhance and expand cultivation, to help cultivators buy seeds and opt for commercial farming. In fact, so seductive was the possibility of huge profits that the Governor of Bombay reported that every piece of land 'within reach of the sea wall will be laid down this season with nothing but cotton'. Wacha put it even more eloquently:

> All classes of persons, even those with hardly a hundred rupees in their pockets, went in hot pursuit of obtaining cotton, rubbish or any other, and it was said, perhaps, with a tinge of exasperation, that even beddings were ransacked and eagerly cut open to collect the cotton in order that a few thousand seers of such stuff may find a profitable mark to rejoice the heart of these humble 'dealers'.[30]

The cotton rush set the stage for Premchand Roychand's exploits in speculation, both, in cotton, and with its proceeds, in land-reclamation schemes. Backing his ventures was the Bank of Bombay whose interests in cotton speculation led to major relaxations in the policy of credit advances. This in a large measure was the result of the growing partnership of the bank with Premchand Roychand and his father who was known to undertake the business dealings of important bank officials. In this context the resignation[31] of Sir Cowasjee Jehangir from the bank proved disastrous as the new officials, persuaded by Premchand, initiated a policy of reckless advances and speculation—initially in cotton and subsequently in land reclamation. The idea of investing in reclamation was not new in Bombay but the urgency with which it began to be carried out now was unprecedented. Personal considerations and calculations outweighed official policy and caution as reckless speculation ensued. The secretary of the Bank of Bombay, James Blair, initiated a new policy of making advances without proper securities and also began to discount promissory notes signed by a single borrower without taking additional security.[32] In this, Blair, like so many of his colleagues at the bank and outside, was reacting to the growing speculation in cotton and land-reclamation schemes, with the interest in the latter having an older history.[33]

Schemes related to land reclamation and civic infrastructure were part of the history of Bombay city's growth and municipal development. From the beginning of the nineteenth century the city's officials as well as merchant investors were interested in urban improvement and reclamation schemes.[34] Ever since the city started showing signs of commercial expansion and escalating demand for space, proposals for reclaiming submerged lands came forth with increasing regularity. The earliest comprehensive plan of reclamation was prepared in 1843 by Col G.R. Jervis which interested both the government and the public, and as such set the stage for future private–public partnerships.[35] The first mention of a private land-reclamation company being formed was made in 1837, while in 1857 the Mody Bay Land Reclamation Scheme was put forward. None of these early schemes were able to make much headway because of financial constraints and differences in opinion with the Supreme Government—the foremost seat of the government situated in Fort William, Calcutta. The Apollo Bay Reclamation Scheme was another venture that enjoyed only piecemeal funding partly because of the fear that land prices could fall steeply. However, all this changed in the 1860s as the new Governor of the city Sir Bartle Frere assumed power and charge precisely when cotton speculation brought in unexpected capital flows into the city.[36] Not only was Frere able to convince his superiors that the reclamation schemes could go through, he also made public his conviction that private companies ought to be included in the reclamation schemes for they would work better than the public ones. As he pointed out to the authorities in London:

> It is this uncertainty which makes me despair of ever getting much of these profitable reclamations done by government on their own account. In a general way, a rupee spent in reclamation near the Town yields Rs 3 worth of land—if the work be well planned, and well and quickly done. But the capital required is large and if we have nothing to spend, but what we can clip from canals in Sind or cotton roads in Deccan, our

reclamation get on but slowly—and because slowly, very expensively, for slower the work, the more costly it is, the returns are longer postponed, and interest accumulates on capital sunk.[37]

These schemes drew even more public attention in the wake of the cotton speculation. Not only did the cotton trade bring huge amounts of cash into the city, it foregrounded the issue of transportation and infrastructural improvements that were necessary for trade. At the same time it encouraged the formation of multiple financial institutions, corporations and reclamation companies. Existing institutions like the Bank of Bombay were convinced about the schemes and consequently began to press for greater access to funds and were prepared to extend financial assistance without reliable securities in the hope of making more profits. By the early 1860s the demand for cash was insatiable—as Walter Cassels a leading merchant observed:

> . . . notwithstanding such large importations the demand for money has so far exceeded production that serious embarrassment has ensued and business has almost come to a standstill from the scarcity of the circulating medium. As fast as rupees have been coined, they have been taken into the interior and have there speedily disappeared from circulation, either in the Indian substitute for the stocking foot or in the smelting pot for conversion into bangles.[38]

For immediate amelioration paper currency was introduced although it could only be issued by the government. Private banks were denied this right but they went full steam ahead with speculation—both in cotton and reclamation. The Bank of Bombay took the lead as it stepped forward, while a series of Acts in 1863 and 1865 lifted certain restrictive provisions regarding the granting of advances and personal securities. This change in policy benefited Premchand and his father who by this time had already secured a firm foothold in the bank's circles by working for several bank officials and directors. They possessed a twofold commercial advantage: one was a set of valuable contacts with cotton agencies in Gujarat that enabled Premchand to exploit the cotton fever more effectively than could others; and the other was a series of intimate and personal connections with the Bank of Bombay and its European associates. The latter were as keen to dabble in speculation and make investments that seemed to promise unprecedented returns. It was this proclivity of investors for amassing quick wealth that Premchand exploited fully to his advantage. In fact the first credit advances seem to have gone to Premchand's father. Then during the governorship (1862–66) of Sir Bartle Frere it was the turn of Premchand himself to enjoy favours: the Governor demonstrated his confidence in Premchand by appointing him as a director in the Bank of Bombay and also encouraged him to launch the Backbay Reclamation Company—even proposing to buy 300 shares in the company to retain control over the venture. This suggestion was not eventually carried through as the government rejected it. Shares were thereafter put up for public auction and what followed was a wave of frenzied speculation, artificially shored up by the broker and his associates—against a face value of Rs 5000 per share, they fetched a colossal sum of Rs 1.06 crore—a premium of Rs 21,500 per share.[39] What followed was the floating of several financial companies and corporations and a share-mania the likes of which the city had not seen before. As Wacha comments:

> First came the flotation of banks followed by the launching of 'financial associations'. These in their turn were followed by an even more formidable and ambitious class of concerns known as khuda or reclamation companies. It became the fashion among the prominent financiers of the day that the most influential bank should have at its elbow an equally influential financial feeder in the form of a financial association and that as a corollary or appendix to both, there should be a powerful reclamation company, popularly christened 'khudo'.[40]

This phenomenon of triangulation—the arrangements among banks, financial corporations and reclamation companies—was what characterized the speculation mania in the 1860s, and Premchand was at the centre of it all. Taking advantage of the influence he enjoyed over the directors of the Bank of Bombay and over other senior merchant houses like that of Ritchie Stuart and Company, and sensing the mood in the city, Premchand enthusiastically participated in the new schemes. The Asiatic Banking Corporation promoted the Financial Association of India and China which in turn launched the Bombay Reclamation Company (Backbay Reclamation) of which Premchand was appointed the head. The way these triangular associations worked was as follows:

when a financial association promoted a reclamation company, it fed the speculation jointly with the bank; the shares of the last would be hypothecated to the first two which in their turn would go in for 'time bargain' sales, i.e., enter into a contract for its sale or purchase at a certain time in the future.[41] This kind of association not only boosted confidence among the city investors—enabling a big jump in share values—but also encouraged the formation of such triangulated associations at the lower levels. As Wacha summed up so perceptively:

> What the first class capitalist and merchant did one day, the second class capitalist and trader did the second day, and so on, in a descending scale. Hence it is a fact that after a time, it became the fashion for anybody and everybody to start a financial scheme, get some speculative brokers gifted with the art of bulling the share scrip, whatever its intrinsic worth, and of recommending all and sundry to go in for that particular concern and realise in a day a considerable fortune.[42]

Thus more and more reclamation companies came into existence, land prices appreciated hugely and a vicious cycle was set in permanent motion. Underlying this expansion were a combination of two processes and tendencies—the speculative imperative and the preoccupation with expansion and infrastructure—which was seen as essential for the growth of the city's commercial prospects. Thus the reclamation of land at Backbay was intended primarily for the Bombay–Baroda and Central Indian Railway, and attracted the investments of several local businessmen. The enthusiasm was endorsed by the Governor who remarked in his characteristic manner: 'I am rather glad to see it undertaken by people on the spot, instead of their being made mere pilot fish to the great sharks of the London share market.'[43]

At the eye of the storm were the Bank of Bombay, the Backbay Company, the Asiatic Banking Corporation (which was set up to look after the Backbay Company) and a whole bunch of new companies that Premchand floated with the tacit endorsement of the Bank of Bombay whose directors were allotted lucrative shares. Companies were started for every imaginable purpose—land reclamation, trading, cotton cleaning, pressing and spinning, coffee and steamers—with the shares of these being sold at a high premium.[44] The Bank of Bombay that had been set up in 1840 and functioned as a conservative institution was transformed in the mid-1860s as its directors entered the speculative market in a big way. Premchand's manipulations and personal connections combined with the speculative interests of the bank directors, meant that all prudence was thrown to the winds. Companies and schemes were floated indiscriminately as they found willing buyers especially small- and mid-sized ones. This was largely because Premchand could build around him an aura of invincibility and success and was able to convince his prospective clients of the enormous fortunes to be made. His connections with the Bank of Bombay enhanced his prestige while neutralizing any possibility of scrutiny. The manner in which he bought over the bank's directors and secretary— Blair in particular—meant that the bank was committed to supporting Premchand's schemes. In order to facilitate

Premchand's and their own investment interests these officials were prepared to compromise on basic banking principles and practices. Thus huge amounts of money were advanced by Blair to Premchand as well as numerous other companies without consulting the other directors of the bank and without any security guarantee except the promissory note of the party. Moreover advances were made for longer periods than the stipulated three months. Indeed in many cases the prospective investors received advances on the strength of Premchand's recommendation from the Bank of Bombay as well as the Asiatic Corporation, and thus were able to acquire shares in the companies promoted by him. His influence and persuasive powers came into full force as he manipulated the Bank officials to allot original shares to his friends and associates in the concerns promoted by him and thus reduced the bank to the status of his personal property. Evidently the negligence and venality of the Bank officials was a contributory factor to the share mania, something which Amiya Bagchi's work on the State Bank of India demonstrates so skilfully.[45] Sylvester Birch, the bank manager, gained from speculation in practically all the leading land-development schemes as also in some of the most audacious schemes for long-term lending (the so-called 'financials'). He procured allotments in several companies which began to be floated around 1863–64. While until 1860 there had been only five joint stock companies with a paid-up capital of Rs 35,59,000, in the early 1860s more than fifty-one companies came into being,[46] most of them again being banks, lending/financial institutions and land-development companies. These were justified as secure investment on account of the interest and enthusiasm demonstrated by the city's Governor and administrators for infrastructural and beautification schemes for the city. What made speculation even more risky was the fact that only a few persons acted as promoters of the major companies and banks, while financial corporations and land-development corporations came to be triangulated, that is, one bank having its own corresponding financial and land-development company, and working in tandem with these. The way the linkages worked to produce a speculation fever was summed up eloquently by Wacha:

> When the old Financial was started, the Asiatic Bank helped to promote its speculation by advancing on its shares. When the Financial in turn promoted the Reclamation Company, it fed the speculation jointly with the Bank. It was something like the stream feeding the rivulet till the rivulet and stream together swelling into a river, outflowed or discharged themselves into the mighty ocean.[47]

Thus it was the start-up Asiatic Banking Corporation—whose shares had been skilfully rigged to a premium of 65 per cent in a few months—which was the forerunner of almost ninety-four other monetary institutions. As Wacha wrote, the first vital spark of speculation that eventually burst into a conflagration was kindled by the Asiatic Banking Corporation, and the chief luminary to ignite the fire and fan it into a flame unmindful of the catastrophe to which it might lead was Premchand Roychand. His audacity alone had the power to persuade the masses who were unaware of what the future held in store for them.[48] The other important element contributing to the emerging share mania was the augmentation of the capital of the Bank of Bombay by the new manager James Blair under whose stewardship the bank's charter was amended and old prohibitions on personal advances were lifted. From this point onwards the most reckless system of advances commenced. Lakhs of rupees were advanced while the documents signed by the borrowers were rudimentary and informal, so much so that the rate of interest provided in case of default was less than that charged during the currency of the loan.[49] These careless procedures opened the doors to laxity and bad banking practices and consequently advances were made on supposed substantial securities with a highly fictitious value. Premchand was undoubtedly at the centre of the speculative frenzy as he used his influence over the Bank officials to determine the course of advances. As the inquiry commission set up later to investigate the causes of the failure of the Bank of Bombay pointed out:

> Intelligent and subtle, Premchund Roychund was not slow to fathom the imbecility and weak moral character of Mr Blair and soon acquired great influence over him and his subordinates with complete command of the funds of the bank. He procured allotments for Blair, and lent him money, and what was much the same thing his father Deepchund Roychund constantly supplied Mr Blair with large sums. Premchund Roychund also bought and sold shares for Mr Blair, and entered into joint speculations with him, and never

charged him a rupee for brokerage. The result was that the bank became Premchund's and he deployed his favours in recommending loans and advances to whomsoever he trusted as friends and associates. The latter became part of an extended network and he used this to access money for his own speculative ventures. Sanctioning loans became part of his activities in the bank and so complete was his control and influence that there was no check to his operations. His influence was felt not only at the head office but at the branches also, the agents at Kalbadevi, Broach and Surat all receiving instructions to consult Premchund or his agents respecting advances.[50]

If the commission was to be believed Premchand hoodwinked the officials at every step, taking full advantage of their own avarice. Speaking to the commission Sorabjee Jamsetjee Jeejeebhoy (a Parsi merchant in Bombay) pointed out how on 19 July 1864 he obtained a cash credit for Rs 5 lakh giving no security other than a promissory note. Acting under Premchand's advice he had made unsuccessful applications for allotments in the Backbay Company to two of its promoters, Cowasjee Jehangir and 'Mr Scott'. In Sorabjee's words:

Premchand called on me to know whether I had received shares from Mr Scott. I replied in the negative. He said, never mind I will manage all that for you and told me to give him a commission to purchase for me as many shares I wished. I told him I was short of money and I could do no more than purchase a few shares. Premchand said—Take my word Sorabjee and do not trouble yourself about money. I will get you as much money as you require. But do not go in for less than 1000 shares. I said yes and asked him how he would manage—he said he would get it from Asiatic and Bombay banks. The next day or day after, he sent me two notes, one addressed to Mr Morrison the manager of the Asiatic Bank and one to the Bank of Bombay. In the latter he requested Mr Blair to accommodate Sorabjee with Rs 5 lakh. The result was that both men did what Premchand asked them to do Eventually, Premchand took cheques from Sorabjee.[51]

The transaction clearly revealed how influential Premchand was and how he was able to arm-twist both Bank officials as well as interested investors into doing what served his interests. There were several such instances, all of which the inquiry commission detailed in its report to state that Premchand 'acted without any sense of responsibility or duty, without honour or principle himself, he corrupted the securities, never disclosed to his brother-directors the business the bank was doing and used its money for his own purposes and to the ruin of the interests of the bank'.[52]

How far was this impression a valid and legitimate one? Certainly it was partly correct—if one goes by contemporary impressions especially of those not directly associated with the speculation it is evident that the hype that was built around the cotton trade and speculation unleashed a kind of madness that was not easily contained. As the eldest son of Jamsetjee Jeejeebhoy observed in a letter dated 13 May 1865 to his friend in London, John Bowman, matters were grim and the chief cause of the existing state of affairs was the undue speculation in shares which took place six months ago when there had been enormous 'speculation in time bargains' over shares in land-reclamation companies'. In another communication dated 23 June he mentioned that the prosperity of Bombay had scaled unnatural heights, and the undue speculation which had raged so fiercely was followed by a backlash: 'There is at this moment a complete collapse in the share markets that has brought ruin to many. My own countrymen will be the heaviest sufferers but all classes of the community more or less suffer.'[53] The inquiry commission endorsed these impressions; in fact some of the allusions to the way in which the nexus between the Bombay merchant and the Bombay banking system worked highlighted how Premchand was able to get away with false securities and capitalize on the lapses that the Bank of Bombay was responsible for.

The commission also implicitly suggested that Premchand was not the sole instigator of poor banking and speculative practices. It stated that Blair too played his role by acting on his own and giving out large loans on personal security. There was no proper evaluation of the securities; subsequent examinations for instance demonstrated how jewels were overvalued and even property estimates were inflated in value. As the inquiry commission pointed out, Blair found scope in the Act of 1865 to have effected radical changes in the practices of the bank related to cash credits for example. Instead of insisting on old practices that relied on government papers, guaranteed rail shares or bullion, Blair had allowed cash advances on personal security—with the first of these advances being offered to Premchand's father. At the same time the Bank of Bombay in terms of its structure and management was defective; in contrast to developments elsewhere in British India the bank's branches were largely unsupervised—the duties of the agents were not specified and a degree of laxity entered important policy decisions regarding advances and securities. Equally unfortunate was the poor quality of managers appointed to the new companies. These were mediocre men for the most part—men, to quote a contemporary newspaper, 'who ought never to have left the desk of a mere clerk'.[54] The case of Pestonji Cursetji Shroff who was involved in the share mania embodied how business was being done at a time when the speculation frenzy blinded people. As Dwijendra Tripathi describes in his account of the insane interlude that the share mania represented in the history of Bombay, Shroff was a clerk with very little skill or foresight. Speculation in cotton and shares brought him some dividends and thanks to his contacts with Premchand he was able to invest money in the Eastern Financial Company. With a thousand shares (bought with the assistance of Premchand) Shroff rigged the market so efficiently that the shares of this company which was once on the verge of bankruptcy were now sold at a 40 per cent premium. Lured by the prospect of profits, other directors of the company offloaded their shares which Shroff duly bought and thus brought the company under his complete control. A similar situation took place with the Mazgaon Reclamation Company and the Alliance Financial, both firms associated with the triumvirate—Dr Driver, George Taylor and Atmaram

Madhavji. These were reclamation companies in which Premchand had originally invested. These were sold to Dr Driver and Co. for a huge profit which only furthered more speculation.[55]

High premiums for shares constituted one important feature of the share mania that raged in Bombay between 1863 and 1864. Time bargain was another feature.[56] The general public was convinced that share prices would continue to go up and voluntarily entered into agreements to sell or purchase shares at prices far above their current value. The result was an unprecedented wave of speculation that did not even consider the possibility of a crash and meltdown. Although there were telltale signs of an inevitable and impending crisis and senior merchants often voiced their concerns, these found no listeners.

The end of the Civil War in the United States changed the situation overnight. It was immediately evident that the resumption of American supplies of cotton would once more support the British industry and that the moment of glory for Indian cotton was over. Gripped by a situation of unprecedented panic the city went berserk as investors rushed to dispose of their shares in the bubble companies—but there were no buyers. The banks and financial companies that had advanced the funds found themselves in a hopeless situation. Tumbling prices, panicky investors and depleted banks embodied the crisis that the city experienced; and predictably enough the edifice built on shares and stocks and bubble companies collapsed like a house of cards.[57] By June 1865 it was impossible to ignore the serious state of affairs.

Leading merchant Rustomjee Jeejeebhoy apprised the government of the crisis. 'I need not tell you,' he wrote, 'that commercial matters in Bombay are at present in a great state of jeopardy. Distrust prevailing everywhere and business is nearly at a standstill, because cash payments are almost suspended.' In fact the younger Jeejeebhoy who had succeeded to his father's title and fortunes stressed again and again how he had scrupulously avoided speculation and that barring his errant brother-in-law, nobody in his family was implicated in what he considered a bad and risky business. His letter to William Ramsay dated 23 June 1865 mentioned the seriousness of the crash, and how his brother and he had nothing to do with it and how unfortunate it was that 'innocent people feel the pressure of this when securities of all kinds have fallen so miserably low as to be scarcely saleable. You may form an idea of the present state of things when I tell you that the Bank of Bombay shares which were nearly 200 per cent premium six months ago are now below par.'[58]

Predictably the money market in Bombay now began to contract and overdue bills on the Bank of Bombay piled up without being realized. Fears of an imminent ruin were voiced and as the Governor of the city acknowledged, 'We are now in the midst of a commercial crisis, more severe probably than ever visited any trading community in time of peace; no description can give an adequate notion of the present state of universal panic and distrust.' By the end of June the situation worsened—overdue bills, crisis of solvency, and the ruin of several families marked what was undoubtedly a dark moment in Bombay's financial history. On 1 July

1865 the day marked for settlement of the time bargains, merchant after merchant declared insolvency and several companies went into liquidation. The first major failure was that of the House of Cama which in turn affected other banks and financial institutions. By the end of the following year the collapse was complete as more than sixty merchants of Bombay had lost over a million rupees in speculation, while the liabilities of twenty-four bankrupt firms alone amounted to Rs 19 crore, with others running up a cumulative loss of Rs 7 crore. As the Bombay Chamber of Commerce mentioned in their annual report of 1865:

> The official year just closed will be notable in the history of Bombay as a year hitherto unparalleled in its commercial annals for the reckless spirit of gambling speculation which resulted to large numbers as might be expected from its character—in utter ruin and disgrace. The unexpected wealth poured into the lap of western India by the terrible incident of the American Civil War—now happily brought to a close—was not used wisely. Two years ago a mania for share speculation broke out, which continued to grow in intensity, till it seemed to absorb the time and attention of the community. The legitimate trade of Bombay was comparatively neglected and the energies of the people devoted to the promulgation of schemes, the utility of which the public was probably the last thing worthy of consideration by the promoters.[59]

Time would now tell who among the investors had the guts and gumption to rise from the ruins and build fortunes anew. It was here that Premchand's natural buoyancy and ability surfaced to stand him in good stead. Even as he was stripped to the bone trying to pay off his creditors and even help the Bank of Bombay to salvage some of its reputation, he demonstrated remarkable resilience in rebuilding himself, his reputation and fortunes.

It was perhaps this aspect of Premchand's character that earned him the abiding respect of contemporaries and later commentators whose tribute never failed to recognize his resilience and readiness to make good his commitments. In fact what is striking about Wacha's account is how he seems to see Premchand as a 'market artiste'—a veritable magician—and his lesser contemporaries like Pestonjee Shroff who seem to have been doing the same thing—as con artists. He stated: 'Premchund was the august light and presence; Mr Shroff the shadow and reflection. Mr Premchund's overpowering influence with the leading monetary bodies and individuals was real and co-extensive with his own colossal transactions.'[60]

Even the inquiry commission in its report stated that Premchand's position was not that of an ordinary speculator and that he was described by some as 'the keystone of Bombay's prosperity'.[61] The commission might have been baffled by this and it would seem that his influence was endorsed by one and all especially by the government. Governor Bartle Frere was supposed to have said that Premchand's status was like nothing that he had ever seen or heard of in any other community. Did this reputation stem from Premchand's charities? Or was it his temperament that charmed one and all? From the vantage point of hindsight it might appear somewhat enigmatic that a merchant who thought nothing of selling dreams and stardust should have been so punctilious in making good his own debts. If Wacha, his biographer, is to be believed, then Premchand and his conduct was symptomatic of traditional business ethos. The moral tone among men of business was supposed to have been so high that it was 'deemed an act of shame and disgrace to deviate by a hair's breadth from the usage of *meum* and *tuum* in commercial transactions'.[62] Was this aspect a feature of caste and caste-related notions of honour? Or was it an inevitable necessity imposed by the mechanisms and modality of pre-modern loan operations that depended so critically on trust and reciprocity? We do know that the reputation of a traditional merchant and trader in India depended very centrally on trust and that money was always lent by word of mouth and that the borrower and lender had to keep their word which was expected to be as good as a bond—signed, stamped and registered. There are innumerable urban legends associated with well-known bankers—for example Atmaram Bhucan whose business practices were considered synonymous with integrity itself in Bazaar Gate Street. More commonly known as the firm of Kaka Parikh (as Atmaram Bhucan was affectionately referred to)—everyone in the city of Bombay knew where it was. Also it was generally agreed that his credit rating was so high that he had to but offer a single hair from his moustache to raise funds from the public. Clearly, Premchand belonged to this world of trust and reciprocity when it came to loan transactions even if his speculation had allowed his good sense to betray him. Risk-taking was accompanied by a willingness to make good his commitments and it was this balance that facilitated his ventures at a time when personal connections and an uncanny ability and disposition to read the market and ride its wave came to be essential ingredients for business transactions.

It now remained for Premchand to begin life all over again—this was what he confessed to his friend Sir George Birdwood who was present in Bombay[63] when the news of the crash came. How he reconstructed his life remains something of a mystery as there is very little factual evidence to go by. In fact the silence that envelops Premchand in official documentation of the government, either during or after the crash, is somewhat baffling. There are however, a number of impassioned retrospective references by his admirers like Wacha and Birdwood to his fortitude and temperament; they commented on his extraordinary energy and resilience and his ability to once more conduct business and even ride the market. We know that faced with the liquidation of his debts and the huge and irrecoverable losses of the Bank of Bombay, the situation was not especially easy. We also know that the crisis initiated a new set of reforms in business organization and practice and that these inaugurated a new era in commerce for the city. Whether Premchand was able to fit into the new system immediately is not known but it is known that his family continued to thrive and that he participated in key civic issues—reflecting an important shift in his orientation. He continued with his business in brokerage and his understanding of shares never failed to impress contemporaries or later commentators. Presumably his investment in real estate acted as a buffer against complete ruin and enabled him to stay afloat. Nor did his reputation take an irreparable beating as he continued to be regarded as a philanthropist whose social commitment was unusual by any standard. In fact, if his biographers are to be believed, his charities expanded even more substantially after the crisis and he began to participate more vocally in civic politics.

To appreciate the philanthropy of Premchand is to actually understand the nature of his larger public engagement as a modern citizen. Beyond the conventional role merchants were known to perform as donors and builders of charities and trusts, Premchand seems to have been especially interested in the idea of dissemination of education as a public good and in safeguarding the welfare of the destitute, both among his community and outside. His extensive endowments to the universities of Bombay and Calcutta reflect an abiding concern for the dissemination of education among Indians. He would appear to have shared a vision for the city of Bombay and for its public space and architecture, one that embodied a notion of progress and improvement. Indeed it is this curious attachment to progress and the disposition to risk that made Premchand what he was and also earned him an enormous amount of goodwill and appreciation from contemporaries, Indians and Europeans like.

Admittedly for a later-day historian it is not always easy to judge and evaluate the actions and personality of a man like Premchand especially through the writings of acolytes and admirers. Wacha and Birdwood were hardly objective and neutral observers—both men had close relations with the grand old broker and their tributes formed part of an urban legend that was built around the success of indigenous capital and the visibility of his philanthropy. The appreciation for men like Jeejeebhoy and Premchand was so strong among their admirers that there seems to have been no sense of disquiet about either the nature and morality of the opium traffic in one case or the reckless speculation that ruined hundreds in the other. How does one explain the silence? How does one recuperate the activities and intentions of individual big players in a larger story on Indian capital and business? It is not an easy task given the nature of the archive which suggests their instinctive alignment with the ruling establishment. Hence it would not be an exaggeration to suggest that in terms of both commerce as well as social values related to charity the merchants were quick to adopt values that came with the rule of the Company and thereafter the Raj. Douglas Haynes in an insightful article on gifting and philanthropy in western India suggests how shifts in the form of mercantile charity have to be understood in the context of imperial rule in the subcontinent. Just as the Raj had a moral obligation towards the progress and upliftment of its subjects, so did the merchants envisage new and expanded roles for themselves. Thus even as colonial officials began to urge wealthy subjects to donate generously, the latter began to see in this opportunities for social and commercial leverage. This is not to suggest that merchants saw charity in purely instrumentalist ways but to make the larger point that they were always on the lookout for strategies that could augment their operations and status.

Even more difficult is to map ethical concerns among vernacular capitalists. How does one understand cultural practices of Indian businessmen in a century of transition when they were still negotiating two diverse spaces embodied in the traditional and in the colonial modern? How did capitalists negotiate social capital with commercial capitalism and the imperatives of doing business? These are questions that do not have easy answers. Yet these need to be asked to make greater sense of the enduring value of caste and kinship networks, religious convictions among Indian business groups who simultaneously negotiated in the backdrop of the ethics of the Anglo-Indian legal system, the British rule and its ideology, to legitimize themselves as modern subjects. This also reveals the distinction between western-style capitalist institutions and the existing credit and trade structure that may loosely be described as the bazaar. These domains were different in terms of structure and practice and even ethos and while being complementary in economic transactions, supported a very different set of notions about public good and civic well-being.

The motives of profit and philanthropy went hand in hand for most of the nineteenth-century businessmen in Bombay.[64] For the Parsis charity-related activities were linked to identity issues that required an explicit demonstration of Indo-British civic values which would establish the primacy of their elite status in the city. Besides there was a genuine concern for improving urban facilities especially water supply and sanitation which also involved a stake in the real estate and reclamation business; at the same time they also articulated their personal philosophy of modern civic responsibility. Thus even in Premchand's case while the investment in urban infrastructure was partly informed by business requirements and preconditions, the charities associated with medical dispensaries and education were not extensions of business although organizationally these were not detached from business models of trusteeship. In January 1865 Premchand was busying himself with setting up a committee for the management of Rs 5 lakh which would go into the establishment of an asylum for the aged, infirm, blind and destitute members of the Bania community. What was interesting about the scheme was the way Premchand wanted it organized, both in terms of its logistics and intention. He expressed his views in a letter to the committee: 'It is my hope that this object be attained without destroying or weakening that independence which is the only security of permanent support and for which the vaniya community is now remarkable, and that the widows and orphans may be housed, the sick tended [to] and the suffering supplied with medical assistance and those temporarily in distress tided over their difficulties.'[65]

The project involved the Bombay government as well, for it was expected to keep Rs 4 lakh as deposit and make over its half-yearly interest to the committee administering the charity and asylum. The site for the asylum was to be the Trawadi estate in Mazgaon. The government responded favourably to these initiatives; in fact the proximity of the city's businessmen to the official administration gave very substantial shape to the development of the city. Premchand's commitment to improving the educational infrastructure of his city was apparent when he immediately responded to Mary Prescot whose school building had been demolished; she was compensated by Premchand who interceded on her behalf with the Bombay government. He continued donating to her school that was set up for girl children. More such initiatives followed—the Bombay Scottish Orphanage and the Alexandra Girls' School being cases in point. Besides in 1865 he contributed to the development of the Asiatic Society by sponsoring the publication of important scholarly work on heritage and architecture.

Premchand's personal interest in property and its beautification explained his civic vision. The manner in which he balanced his traditional roles of charity with a more modern sense of investment in philanthropy does suggest how as a beneficiary and as a figure of transition, Premchand was able to navigate complex cultural spaces and embody the spirit of the colonial modern. The idea and experience of colonial modernity was complex—accommodating as it did the consequences of British rule at institutional and ideational levels, and their reception and transmutation in the hands of colonized subjects. It was thus both a product resulting from external colonial pressure and from the urge to self-fashion oneself within a selected traditional sphere.

Premchand Roychand breathed his last in August 1906. By this time the situation was no longer what the young Premchand had encountered and grown up in. His life had been witness to some of the headiest days of trade and speculation that the city had experienced. This era also saw the urban growth and transformation of Bombay. The period of his retirement from active business on the other hand, had seen a fundamental change in the social fabric of commerce where regulations and new legislations had changed the terms of business. British law as it had existed had rather unclear provisions with regard to public disclosure of business details of a joint stock company. There was no provision for a mandatory submission of an auditor's report while the balance sheet contained data of a generalized kind. Investors had little legal protection, the absence of which had clearly manifested during the share crisis. Thus the Company's Act of 1866 came as a useful corrective as it made it incumbent on directors to show an annual balance sheet and place it along with the auditor's report before an annual general meeting. Alongside came the greater regulation of banks with the promulgation of the Presidency Banks Act of 1876. How Premchand Roychand responded to these changes is not clear. The references of his operations after the crash are few and far between and only occasionally allude to his participation in the bazaar that emerged as a very distinct space from the upper echelons of the colonial economy. He did not, for instance, invest in the manufacturing sector that became so important in late nineteenth-century Bombay and Ahmedabad. His interests seem to have been firmly focused on brokerage and the share market. His philanthropic activities on the other hand reflected a rare expansiveness and commitment that embraced education, the arts and public welfare. He was part of the growing business fraternity that held a definite vision for the city in terms of its public face, both in terms of architecture and by way of civic amenities. The participation in philanthropy was not just a part of social responsibilities that augmented self-worth in relation to the immediate community, but also an expression of a public stand—a position that factored in not only status but also a complex engagement with the idea and requirements of capitalist modernity.

The obituaries that followed the death of Premchand Roychand predictably stressed his extreme financial sagacity and his placid temperament which knew how to handle crisis and prosperity alike, and also his unstinted generosity. Both Birdwood and Wacha spoke about his cheerful countenance which was 'no mean element in the magnetic attention he drew towards himself. Even when bowed down by adversity that cheeriness was still to be perceived in a subdued form.'[66] Birdwood described him as the greatest benefactor that Bombay had known: 'the bravest and best of men'. It was a eulogy that certainly spoke of his courage when the chips were down and in all probability it was the same courage that had persuaded the young man to take the risk of creating a bubble and making impossible speculations. Nor was the decision entirely irrational. As far as the broker was concerned he could count on the support of the British community and the administration, the willing cooperation of local brokers, and on his own intimate knowledge of the market. Thereafter the speculation fever seems to have taken over, and aided and abetted by a small circle of bank officers and European traders he took the plunge—finally to suffer a resounding debacle. So while the share mania represented in every sense an insane interlude, it also spoke of a particular moment in the history of the city and its tryst with a volatile market which responded to a series of global trends and pulls. It also reflected the nature of the business fraternity in Bombay which was far more cosmopolitan than its eastern counterpart. The close association of Indians with European merchants and agency houses had always been a feature of Bombay's business world. Well into the first three decades of the nineteenth century Indian merchants had operated alongside European private merchants and even after, there was a greater level of cordiality between local merchants and the government. The Indian merchants along with members of a small group of European agency houses with whom they were often intimately connected as brokers and business partners, formed 'a remarkably close knit oligarchy'—as described by Asiya Siddiqi[67]—which governed the island's trade practices both domestically and overseas. The proximity of this connection was apparent in Premchand's life and career and also enabled Bombay businessmen to continue participation in business, including export trade, with greater confidence. The trajectories of the careers of Dwarkanath Tagore in Calcutta and Jamsetjee Jeejeebhoy and Premchand Roychand in Bombay highlight the contrast between colonial Calcutta and Bombay, and the very different ways in which partnerships worked. Thus during the high noon of imperialism, even when Bombay businessmen faced the brunt of increasing European domination, indigenous business groups were able to retain strong positions in the field of trade and exchange. The strength came from a variety of factors—locational, historical and individual. The fact that business groups in the region enjoyed traditional reserves of capital and credit which were firmly embedded in the political economy of the region and that their resources were seen as critical by the new colonial power was important. Admittedly the trade cycle in different commodity markets was also an important factor that enabled business groups and individuals like Premchand to capitalize on the upswings of commodity trade in cotton and opium.

These broad speculations may still not be enough to explain the success and vitality of indigenous business enterprise or the talents of a broker like Premchand. History has known remarkable men of talent who exhibited that extra ounce of energy to emerge as kings of the market. Some among them had advantages of accumulated wealth and experience while others had opportune moments to test their skills. What united them was perhaps a strong sense of adventure and romance that was associated with commerce and with the exercise of predicting, forecasting and risk-taking. It was the challenge of risks that provided the adrenalin and the rationale to embark upon a cause. Risk-taking was not simply a matter of reasonable calculation but a temperament that was sharpened and honed by training and apprenticeship which could in turn either strengthen or subdue it. In the case of the protagonist the circumstances proved especially fortuitous as events unfolded in a rapid sequence that enabled him to dream of a venture which went far beyond logical calculation.

The spirit of such enterprise persisted through the period of the nineteenth and twentieth centuries, encouraging men of capital and commerce in the region to try their luck in ventures both within and outside India.

Finally, from the perspective of Roychand's experience, one may also reflect on the relationship between capital and land, and on the close connections that were developing among trade, business and real estate. The investment Roychand made in property and real estate was evidently of some importance. Not only did it stand him in good stead, it also lent a particular vision to his subsequent projects of public good. The investment in land was in itself not unprecedented—commercial groups were known to buy land and invest in real estate. How this pattern of investment influenced entrepreneurial decisions or orientation is difficult to ascertain but certainly calls for some reflection. Was this seen as an essential precondition to security and status? Did the pattern of settlement in Bombay enable business groups to develop properties and evolve a civic sense more successfully than they would have elsewhere? Did this reinforce their alignment with the ruling administration in order to articulate an ideology of progress and self-improvement which found expression in public charities and philanthropy? For as understood from a number of recent writings, colonial Bombay was a joint enterprise of Indian elites and European colonials, and the local and the global were both determinate forces in the city's configuration. Speculation and philanthropy went hand in hand and merchant subjects deployed their characteristic wisdom in ensuring that public deals went through to the mutual advantage of the private and public domains. As Preeti Chopra demonstrates in her work on Bombay,[68] taxpayers, landlords, intellectuals and merchants who participated in global commodity exchanges were the principal agents recasting the public–municipal policies conducive to the aid of capitalistic development. The state functioned closely with its merchant subjects; Chopra refers to several instances of private–public partnership that involved merchants and the state coming together in the common cause of civic improvements. These were not always smooth transactions; there are references to a case involving Jamsetjee Jeejeebhoy who was discovered to have illegally built on land by encroaching upon public space in the Fort area—the land in question belonging to Mehrabai, the widow of Hormusjee Cursetjee Shroff. Jamsetjee denied the allegation but subsequent inquiries proved him wrong. The government however, preferred to back its merchant-collaborator and in view of the services provided by the 'Honourable Parsee' it allowed him to retain the land.[69] The instance is important as it does raise the issue of real estate being a prime object of capital in India, as well as the matter of inner contradictions within the emerging articulation of public space and private entitlement.

Seen from this vantage point the figures of Jamsetjee Jeejeebhoy and Premchand Roychand appear remarkably similar. Both had close associates within the ruling circle, both came from humble and modest backgrounds, both made prodigious fortunes and both developed a keen sense of commitment to the city and the order it represented. Both men absorbed the ideology of the ruling class and presented themselves in a manner that made them acceptable to it. Private philanthropy had always been a major resource the government drew on in its attempts to develop Bombay city. Right from the beginning when tanks and wells were built with the contribution of private individuals, to the era of great speculation and reclamation associated with Frere and Roychand, philanthropy had been a key element in the configuration of the city. The transformation of the city's landscape in the wake of the share mania was a turning point when the urban landscape changed decisively with a new cluster of buildings coming up and constituting the Elphinstone Circle. Elphinstone Circle was built entirely on the speculation of the 1860s in which Premchand Roychand had played such a critical role. Chopra refers to the involvement of the city architect Forjett in the speculative scheme and how he was recompensed for his efforts.[70] Businessmen turned to real estate—both Jamsetjee and Roychand did exactly that, as a result of which the urban arena emerged as a site for philanthropy and politics. The emergence of the urban arena as a location for philanthropy had important implications as this ensured a particular mode of private–public partnership in Bombay city's development— traces of which remain today albeit in an altered context.

EPILOGUE

THE ROMANCE OF COMMERCE

WE HAVE TRACKED the life and times of three merchants. All three of them worked in what can conveniently be called 'a time of transition', although in each of these cases the idea of transition had several registers—temporal, social and political. While Trawadi Arjunji Nathji lived through a period of a major political transition, namely from *Pax Mughalica* to *Pax Britannica*, Jamsetjee Jeejeebhoy and Premchand Roychand participated in the emerging colonial economy through its various stages of articulation and in the process displayed their commitment to a new order that colonial Bombay embodied. What made each of them so important and distinctive was the fact that they were exemplary representatives of the times they lived in, who were able to keep step with the changes they witnessed in their lifetimes. If Trawadi Arjunji Nathji calculated that backing the English East India Company would fetch him better returns on capital loaned and would enable a huge expansion in banking operations it was surely a decision that was as much based on an accurate political forecast as it was on an appreciation of what the Company connection could guarantee in terms of protection of property and of business practices. And yet he could not and did not entirely buy into the new ethos of the English order—his social self was firmly grounded in traditional concepts of caste status, honour and religion, with the result that his crossover to the new dispensation was incomplete. Not so with the other two protagonists.

Both Jamsetjee Jeejeebhoy and Premchand Roychand were quintessentially mid-nineteenth-century men of commerce that colonial Bombay spawned and supported. Living and working in Bombay when the city took off—thanks to its fortuitous association with opium and raw cotton—was what defined the operations of the two men, who it must be admitted, had prepared themselves to make a set of right moves. Having taken up residence in a city whose commercial profile was constituted by networks of Indian and European capital working in tandem they developed close links of trust and friendship with important European associates which served them in good stead for the business they embarked upon. For Jamsetjee this marked the beginning of an immensely productive venture that raised the bar for Indian export trade operations. It was not that Indians had not traded overseas in a big way either before Jamsetjee or after him but the fact remains that he more than anyone else was able to break into the international ring of trade that connected India with England directly, and led the way for Indians to participate along with major European players in export trade, shipping and international remittances. This was no mean achievement representing as it did a major advance for Indian overseas trade and capital formation which was subsequently yoked to the preservation of the colonial order whose values Jamsetjee Jeejeebhoy and his son Cursetjee Jeejeebhoy entirely endorsed.[1] In the senior Jamsetjee's case there does not seem to have been any sense of ambivalence in his orientation towards or in his advocacy of those liberal values that British rule represented as these enabled a new regime where private property and commercial practices were safeguarded by law and a new notion of public and civic good was being put in place. This did not mean that Jamsetjee did not face the effects of asymmetry embedded in the colonial system—it is well known that he could not stand up to the competition of global financial power. However, it would be short-sighted to assume that his operations were of a purely comprador variety, that his loyalty bordered on a variety of crony capitalism and that servility was the strategy he adopted for business success. The facts are more complex than such simple reductionism. What appears striking is the complete confidence the 'Honourable Parsee' seems to have had in prosecuting his business ventures which were as wide-ranging in their sweep as they were intricate in detail at the lower levels of supply and procurement. It was as though he could command the heights of the trading world from the uppermost echelons normally reserved for European private traders and simultaneously navigate the messy and muddled bylanes of distribution centres operated by equally powerful syndicates of indigenous businessmen. His commitment to local smaller traders' claims especially in the aftermath of the

Opium Wars (1839–42) was exemplary as he effectively deployed the rhetoric of his masters to insist on quick compensation. As he wrote to his associate Captain Elliot in London on 26 March 1842 saying how callous the government was in ignoring 'the misery and distress that withholding vast sums of money have brought upon the natives of this country. We are too distant from the Home Government to make our voices heard and right and justice appear in our case to be set aside altogether. Nothing is conceded to us, not even promise of future payment and unless you my good sir will stir yourself on our behalf, I fear that we shall never see the day of payment.'[2]

What is striking about this representation was both its self-confident tone as well as its positioning within the existing political structure which enabled the senior trader to enforce monetary claims within a paradigm of rights and entitlement. In the process of and as a result of such negotiation Jamsetjee was able to fashion himself almost entirely in the mould of his colonial masters, sharing their vision of a magnificent and powerful city wedded to ever-expanding commerce and the betterment of its less affluent sections. Admittedly he never questioned the powerful rhetoric of progress and development, believing as he did in the inherent fairness of British rule. He was not alone in holding such an opinion— Premchand Roychand entertained the same confidence in colonial Bombay and its rulers, and so did Trawadi Arjunji Nathji half a century earlier even if then the preoccupation was more with immediate political security rather than with a particular notion of bourgeois respectability and public good.

The close alignment of merchants with state power in India especially during the century of transition and thereafter raises a number of obvious questions. One, can merchants be legitimately seen as unpatriotic and as agents who were entirely and merely guided by pragmatic considerations that could ensure them and their operations a level of security? Two, how critical was the role of the state in developing proto-capitalism in India? And finally how can one explain merchant success? Can it be ascribed only to the contingent factors that British rule produced? Or was there something about the Indian commercial ethos especially in western India where commerce assumed elements of adventure and romance which persuaded many of them to take up commercial ventures at home and overseas and invest thereafter in global commerce and industry?

That merchants emerged as major agents and actors in the century of transition when centralized Mughal power gave way to a fragmented and parcelled-out power structure is well known in recent historiography. The merchants' ability to harness funds, combined with skills in revenue administration and scribal practices meant they were poised to play a key role in the new fiscal arrangements which buttressed the emerging regional states in the subcontinent. Moreover they had at their command sophisticated fiduciary instruments that facilitated the transfer of large funds across borders which financed both trade and warfare.[3] Under these circumstances their disposition to support one power over the other—a choice that was determined by practical considerations of protecting their investments—meant that the question of patriotic identification did not arise at all. There may have been a general identification with a regional power base and polity but in a situation of fragmented political authority the merchants were quick to assess the relative advantages of a particular power in question. In the mid-eighteenth century it was the English power that held the balance and by the end of the century most merchant groups had clearly committed their purse strings to imperial conquest and expansion. It was a connection that held fast until the emergence of Gandhi and his clarion call for freedom. Till then merchants and bankers remained firmly on the side of the new rulers. The connection was oiled not merely by the declared solvency of the Company with its access to the rich revenues of Bengal but also by the strategy it adopted of protecting merchants from the exactions of their rivals. The rhetoric of free and untrammelled trade for the Company and its protégés could not but make an impact on the merchants, and its benefits were augmented by some of the institutions that reinforced early colonial rule. The Mayor's Court was one such institution (set up in the three colonial cities of Madras, Bombay and Calcutta) where Indian merchants found that their disputes could be resolved by law which was not entirely impervious to the workings of local custom as well. The Company was seen to be the protector of property and the custodian of security—factors that were crucial for merchants to carry out their business. Little surprise then that they would en masse become steadfast allies of the new order. In fact even after the bankers were shorn of their traditional resources after 1818 when British paramountcy eroded their traditional functions of revenue handling, coinage and military–political fund transfers, their ties of attachment and loyalty remained strong, so much so that in 1857 patriotism for the Banias and Parsis meant 'fidelity to the British Crown'. Thus Jamasetjee, in acknowledgement of the coin he received from the British Government in honour of his patriotism, observed, 'I shall hand down this medal to my children's children with pride and reverence.'[4] For him British rule was synonymous with liberality and justice in their real and substantial forms. In fact he went so far as to say that the conferment of honours and baronetcy on him broke down barriers that had long separated European and native communities. As he put it: 'I may venture to say that the mark of distinction now so graciously conferred on me will be hailed with universal delight and with feelings of the deepest gratitude to those who advised and recommended it. Foreign nations will also view with pleasing wonder the fostering care bestowed by England upon her colonies and the advancement of her native subjects and will also learn more fully to comprehend the unbounded goodness of the sovereign of that mighty country.'[5]

His Bania counterparts did not articulate their appreciation in quite the same way—but for them too, colonial rule spelt order and security which gave them the wherewithal to conduct their business and to safeguard their property. Every time there was an altercation that threatened to undermine property rights, and law and order, the Bania association reminded their masters about their responsibilities and how they had come to see the colonial order as a bastion of security. This is not to suggest that the coercive and discriminatory policies adopted by the colonial state did not hurt the economic interests of the Hindu and Bania traders who did when necessary express their dissatisfaction; but the point is that the community by and large preferred to throw in its lot with the new order which was seen not merely as balanced but which also gave it the necessary sense of security as well as leverage.

The question thus emerges: to what extent were state structures and their development critical for merchants' success and capital accumulation? Evidently capital accumulation and acceleration of economic forces were long-term processes wherein the state played an important part in many different ways. If the Mughal state had been responsible for ensuring a century and more of political security and infrastructural efficiency (in the form of highway networks and roads, coinage purity etc.), then the post-Mughal scenario had been instrumental in promoting merchants as prime movers of the revenue administration. It was in the eighteenth century that regional states intensified the drive for cash revenues that served to bring merchants even closer to revenue administration. As more and more revenues came to be farmed out and as the states began to increasingly rely on large-scale transfer of funds across borders merchants came into their own and became key figures in the new political configuration of late Mughal India. Here merchant groups from what Claude Markovits calls 'dry zones' enjoyed clear advantages and developed critical commercial skills. Merchants from these areas honed their financial skills rapidly as they had to operate in uncertain conditions which then led to the early development of the futures market in crops.[6] In Rajasthan, for instance, this tendency is well documented. It is not surprising that it was in this region that the hundi network originated and that merchant bankers from here dominated the financial sector in Hindustan. Their dominance over the pan-Indian banking scene was in large part due to the political connections they forged with the rulers; G.D. Sharma in an important work on the Rajput polity referred to the practice of appointing moneylenders to deal with revenue at the lower levels of administration. Thereafter under the Mughal rule merchants became commissars for the army and thus made the important move of extending their links across the subcontinent. Combining this with other commercial activities the merchant communities spread far and wide, never once discounting the importance of political security and patronage. As Markovits observes, 'The ability of Hindu and Jain merchants of the dry zone to use their links with Rajputs to establish some connection to Mughal grandees and rulers is probably one of the keys to the apparent paradox of an unparalleled expansion of Hindu merchant networks under a Muslim regime.'[7]

The eighteenth century and early nineteenth century enabled these groups to further consolidate their position. Even as conditions of insecurity and conflict destabilized the all-India trading network in the eighteenth century the articulation and consolidation of regional political systems enabled the merchant groups to dominate the revenue and fiscal administration and thereafter to align themselves with

the new power—the Company whose discourse on fair trade
and the safeguarding of property commanded a great deal of
appeal. So not surprisingly, when it came to scripting their
history in the twentieth century, the merchant communities
framed it in terms of the political patronage and the state
support they received in guarding their capital. Thus even
when the colonial state had substantially reduced the influence
of local banking groups it still held out prospects for business
groups especially in western India who skilfully adapted
themselves to the new situation, working with the state and
bypassing it whenever possible. There was no question of
subverting the authority of the colonial state that was seen as
the mover of major projects and the custodian of security.
This was of course particularly true of the Parsis, and as
Jamsetjee Nasserwanjee Tata (1839–1904), one of the first
advocates of Indian economic independence wrote:

> Our small community is, to my thinking, peculiarly
> suited as interpreters and intermediaries between the
> rulers and the ruled in this country. Through their
> peculiar position they have benefited more than any
> other class by English rule, and I am sure their gratitude
> to that rule is, as it ought to be, in due proportion to the
> advantage derived from it ... Pure Natives of this
> country, whenever they venture to criticize the actions
> of individuals in authority, are liable to have their
> motives questioned; but in the case of Parsees such
> doubtful motives must be regarded as non-existent.[8]

What needs to be added to this comment is that the Bombay
city was a space with a difference and held certain locational

advantages for business groups like Parsis and Gujarati Banias to operate in tandem with the Europeans. Western India was arguably the most advanced economic region in the subcontinent and furthermore the late arrival of British rule allowed for resilience, and the renewal of older structures and practices. The relatively smaller presence of the British was also an important factor. Amalendu Guha refers to two interesting, even if stray, sets of figures. One is the official return printed on 25 February 1830 of the European civil servants who numbered 237 in the Bombay Presidency, as against 731 and 388 in the Bengal and Madras Presidencies respectively. Earlier figures show a similar break-up suggesting that there was more room for indigenous capital in western India.[9] Additionally European racist discrimination was not as strong in Bombay as in Calcutta, and more importantly, sources of capital and entrepreneurial motivations were not so easily displaced and deflected by volatile trade swings, a feature of the colonial economy. Unlike the case in colonial Calcutta the number of casualties in any period of crisis in Bombay was never too many or even irreversible. Apart from this resilience which one may attribute to social, sociological and historical factors there was also a greater degree of innovative capabilities that distinguished the capitalist class in Bombay from the rest. The island city had a great many firsts—a shipyard and master builders as well as modern finance and large-scale industry, not to speak of great transport and liner companies. This is not to fetishize the exceptionalism of Bombay and its businessmen but to try and make sense of a history where state and subjects worked to meet the dreams of a development story which interestingly also had its detractors in personages like Dadabhai Naoroji and Jamsetjee Tata.

The role of the colonial state in shaping the nature and level of the Indian economy has been a matter of considerable debate. Nationalist critics of British rule like R.C. Dutt and Dadabhai Naoroji emphasized the destructive aspects of British rule and these have constituted the basis for a left-nationalist paradigm for understanding Indian economic history under colonial rule. We have had subsequent revisionist re-evaluations that have through micro-studies suggested the differential impact of British policies in certain regions. Western India, in terms of its economic and business history, certainly represented an important test case as business groups here were able to capitalize on older networks of credit, capital and trust; it was also a test case on the nature of Indo-British commercial partnership that evolved here. Consequently even when the colonial trading economy was fully articulated the bankers and merchants were in a position to both fulfil certain crucial intermediary functions. These functions were middle-tiered ones connecting export operations with agricultural production, the financing and marketing of which was the preserve of Indian merchants especially Bania groups. The same merchants responded to global developments caused by the rise of Japan, and by global flow of commodities connecting discrete economies in the Indian Ocean. Thus Dwijendra Tripathi quite categorically suggests that British rule did not undermine the entrepreneurial operations of Indians; instead he states that changes and small improvements in infrastructure enabled the effective articulation of business and trading operations. Admittedly at least in western India traditional business groups were able to respond to the changing situation and take full advantage initially of the political security that the British rule embodied and subsequently to work both within the system as well as outside it. It is, however, important to stress the fact that it was traditional business and commercial groups like the Banias and Nagar Brahmins in Gujarat who were at the forefront of the commercial drive and who capitalized on their traditional assets of familial ties, information and credit reserves. Of course as scholars like Claude Markovits have pointed out, in relation to circulation and capital flows in South Asia, trust was not an automatic or inevitable function or corollary of caste- or kin-related activities—it was in fact an outcome of demonstrable reputation and accumulated merchant skills, the effects of which were incremental over generations. Organization was also an important asset—the fact that merchant networks evolved specific structures to keep costs low and to circulate the latest information on market developments was significant. Partnerships and systems of agency enabled commercial groups to ramify their operations and helped in the integration of markets. Other communities in Gujarat followed suit as one sees a marked increase in overseas migrations—the case of Lohanas and Bhatias from Kutch being an instance in point. Supplanting the Bhatias they retained a prominent position in the trade of the western-Indian Ocean. The Kutchi miracle—a subset of Gujarat's maritime pre-eminence—is not easy to explain; it could be that Gujarati commercial groups had over time developed a kind of migratory orientation that was fuelled by a love for adventure which money-making seemed to embody. Historically, in Gujarat, traders and financiers enjoyed social pre-eminence—a feature that observers like Abbe Dubois and Georges Roques were quick to notice and which over time was consolidated by a close alliance with the political power of the day. An important consequence of formal British rule was also that it generated mobility within the subcontinent and within the larger space of empire, and subsequently facilitated the coherence of a class formation.

A recent work on Kalidas Nanji Mehta (the East African business magnate) and his exploits suggest that the idea of romance associated with commerce was an important part of the business ethos that had become fairly entrenched by the end of the nineteenth century. The fact was that the British empire enabled business groups to move across vast oceanic spaces with greater freedom thereby generating new opportunities which commercial groups and individuals were able to take advantage of. The building of railways in East Africa held important prospects for Gujarati businessmen who did not flinch at the thought of travelling; they deployed their business contacts in order to secure capital and set up important industrial ventures in Kenya and Uganda. Mehta's autobiography[10] suggests that the willingness to travel, take risks and tap into a variety of contacts were all part of that disposition which had been nurtured over generations. It was this combination that explained both the merchant-capitalist's extreme discipline and attachment to convention and also his ability to grab opportunities with both hands. Whether it was travelling overseas to unfamiliar climes or it was a question of doggedly pursuing accounts, the Bania seemed fascinated by the prospect of money-making; while he responded in his own way to philanthropy and the care of the self.

One other question that remains to be asked is related to the idea of class and community. This study has had its focus on three individuals—exceptional men whose personal experiences and commercial practices while grounded within a defined community set-up had the hallmarks of individual impulse and talent. Can one legitimately use their experiences to make a general set of propositions about the formation of class? Admittedly all three protagonists embodied the eccentricities and characteristics of the context they lived and operated in and were part both of an older community formation as well as of a new one that looked at commercial interests from a more inclusive perspective. One could legitimately argue that associations like the Bania Mahajan had existed even in the early modern period and that these stood for the interests of all commercial groups irrespective of caste divisions and subdivisions, and that there was nothing substantively new about either Jamsetjee speaking on behalf of his less-privileged friends and associates, or Premchand taking up the case of smaller brokers and dealers. And yet the scale had changed substantively—the changes that accompanied colonial trade and power had accelerated the possibilities for mobility and greater class cohesion. The nineteenth century witnessed a rapid transformation of the economy in structural and quantitative terms and generated a wide range of options for new entrants to business and trade and industry. This was exemplified by the experience of the Parsi community in general and Jamsetjee in particular, not to speak of traders like Premchand Roychand or Rancchodlal Chhotalal and Nanji Kalidas from Gujarat and Cutch who came from diverse backgrounds, yet collectively represented the articulation of a new capitalist formation, of a new class that was characterized by an undue dependence on foreign capital, and heavily committed to trade rather than to manufacture. Predictably the business groups did not question the first principles of the colonial economy and they negotiated on these for the best possible opportunities. Thus they responded positively to what they saw as rational inputs in prosecuting business. Indeed by overlooking the moral aspects of a trade in narcotics, which they perceived as entirely legitimate, they used it as a springboard for expansion and consolidation. Emerging as adventurous traders they became and remained gentlemen-capitalists who partook of complex modern ideas, thanks to their location in a cosmopolitan city that was pluralistic, competitive and capital-friendly.

NOTES

Prologue

1. C.A. Bayly, *Rulers, Townsmen and Bazaars: North Indian Society in the Age of British Expansion, 1770–1870* (Cambridge: Cambridge University Press, 1983), pp. 8–10 (hereinafter cited as *Rulers, Townsmen and Bazaars*). *See* Lakshmi Subramanian, *A History of India, 1707–1857* (New Delhi: Orient Blackswan, 2010). *See* Introduction.

2. Muzaffar Alam, *The Crisis of Empire in Mughal North India: Awadh and the Punjab, 1707–1748* (New Delhi: OUP, 1986), p. 38.

3. C.A. Bayly, *Rulers, Townsmen and Bazaars*, pp. 16–19.

4. Ibid., pp. 20–21.

5. Stewart Gordon, *The Marathas: 1600–1818, The New Cambridge History of India* (Cambridge: Cambridge University Press, 1993), pp. 16–17.

6. Ibid.

7. C.A. Bayly, *Rulers, Townsmen and Bazaars*, p. 27.

8. Peter Marshall, *East Indian Fortunes: The British in Bengal in the Eighteenth Century* (Oxford: Clarendon Press, 1976), pp. 9–10, 21–22 (hereinafter cited as *East Indian Fortunes*).

9. H.V. Bowen, *The Business of Empire: The East India Company and Imperial Britain, 1756–1833* (Cambridge: Cambridge University Press, 2006), pp. 7–13, 19–28. *See* Tirthankar Roy, *The East India Company: The World's Most Powerful Corporation* (New Delhi:

Penguin Books India, 2012). Ray's work details the rise of the Company, its composition and evolution through the seventeenth and eighteenth centuries when it not only became the greatest corporation in the world but also became heir to the Mughal empire in India.

10. Ashin Dasgupta, 'Trade and Politics in Eighteenth Century India' in *The World of the Indian Ocean Merchants, 1500–1800: Collected Essays of Ashin Dasgupta*, comp. Uma Dasgupta (New Delhi: OUP, 2001), pp. 140–79.

11. We have a number of important writings on the Company settlements of Bombay, Madras and Calcutta, all of which comment on the fortifications that the Company introduced into the settlements as well as the segregation of white and black towns. *See* Kanakalatha Mukund, *The View from Below: Indigenous Society, Temples and the Early Colonial State in Tamilnadu, 1700–1835* (New Delhi: Orient Blackswan, 2005), pp. 10–20. *See* Lakshmi Subramanian, *Indigenous Capital and Imperial Expansion: Bombay, Surat and the West Coast* (New Delhi: OUP, 1996), pp. 50–51, 78–80; Peter Marshall, *East Indian Fortunes,* pp. 24–26 and Amar Farooqi, *Opium City: The Making of Early Victorian Bombay* (Gurgaon: Three Essays Collective, 2006), pp. 28, 52 . *See* M.D. David, *History of Bombay, 1661–1708* (Bombay: University of Bombay, 1973, pp. 188–200, 262–65). David's work identifies the major stages in the development of Bombay in the eighteenth century, when the Company authorities attempted to improve fortifications and encourage migrants to come and settle down.

12. Claude Markovits, *Merchants, Traders, Entrepreneurs: Indian Business in the Colonial Era* (New Delhi: Permanent Black, 2008), pp. 128–52.

13. K.N. Chaudhuri, 'Foreign Trade and the Balance of Payments (1757–1947)' in *The Cambridge Economic History of India: Volume II,* eds Dharma Kumar and Meghnad Desai (Cambridge: Cambridge University Press, 1983), pp. 806–07.

1. Merchants and Rulers in the Interstices of Empire

1. Lakshmi Subramanian and Rajat Kanta Ray, 'Merchants and Politics From the Great Mughal to the East India Company' in *Business and Politics in India: A Historical Perspective*, ed. Dwijendra Tripathi (New Delhi: Manohar Publishers, 1991), p. 19 (hereinafter cited as 'Merchants and Politics').

2. Tirthankar Roy, *The Economic History of India: 1857–1947* (New Delhi: OUP, 2000), pp. 10–19; Dwijendra Tripathi, *The Oxford History of Indian Business* (New Delhi: OUP, 2004), pp. 3–4 (hereinafter cited as *The History of Indian Business*); and Rajat Kanta Ray, ed., *Entrepreneurship and Industry in India: 1800–1947* (New Delhi: OUP, 1992), pp. 2–6.

3. Mukund Lath, trans., *Half A Tale: A Study In The Interrelationship Between Autobiography And History* (Jaipur: Rajasthan Prakrit Bharati Sansthan, 1981), verses 75, 224, 298; and Rupert Snell, 'Confessions of a 17th Century Jain Mendicant: The Ardha Kathanak of Banarasidas', *South Asia Research*, vol. 25(1), (2005): pp. 79–104.

4. Dwijendra Tripathi, *The Dynamics of a Tradition: Kasturbhai Lalbhai and His Entrepreneurship* (New Delhi: Manohar Publishers, 1981), pp. 3–5 (hereinafter cited as *The Dynamics of a Tradition*).

5. Rajat Kanta Ray, 'Indian Society and the Establishment of British Supremacy: 1765–1818' in *The Oxford History of the British Empire: Volume II: The Eighteenth Century*, ed. P.J. Marshall (USA: OUP, 2001), pp. 508–30.

6. Ibid., pp. 509–10. See Lakshmi Subramanian, *Indigenous Capital and Imperial Expansion: Bombay, Surat and the West Coast* (New Delhi: OUP, 1996), p. 12 (hereinafter cited as *Indigenous Capital and Imperial Expansion*).

7. Lakshmi Subramanian, *Indigenous Capital and Imperial Expansion*, pp. 180–200, 330–39.

8. Douglas Haynes, 'From Tribute to Philanthropy: The Politics of Gift-Giving in a Western Indian City', *The Journal of Asian Studies*, vol. 46, (1987): pp. 340, 346–48, 350–53.

9. Dwijendra Tripathi, *The Dynamics of a Tradition*, pp. 3–5.

10. Ashin Dasgupta, *Indian Merchants and the Decline of Surat: 1700–1750* (New Delhi: Manohar Publishers, 1994), pp. 49–51, 67–68, 84–88 (hereinafter cited as *Indian Merchants and the Decline of Surat*).

11. Lakshmi Subramanian, 'The Eighteenth Century Social Order in Surat: A Reply and an Excursus on the Riots of 1788 and 1795', *Modern Asian Studies*, vol. 25, no. 2 (1991): pp. 322–23ff.

12. Syed Ali Nawab and Charles Norman Seddon, trans., *Mirat-i-Ahmadi: A History of Gujarat in Persian: Gaekwad's Oriental Series: Supplement,* (Baroda: Baroda Oriental Institute, 1928), p. 116 (hereinafter cited as *Mirat-i-Ahmadi*).

13. Walker of Bowland Papers, 1780–1830 (Acc. No. 2228), 'An Account of Castes and Professions in Gujarat', vol. I, Letters, Reports and Papers, Histories (National Library of Scotland, Edinburgh).

14. Ibid.

15. Ashin Dasgupta, 'Indian Merchants and the Trade in the Indian Ocean c. 1500–1700' in *The Cambridge Economic History of India: Volume. I, c. 1200–1750*, eds Tapan Raychaudhri and Irfan Habib (New Delhi: Orient Longman, 1982), pp. 419–25 (hereinafter cited as 'Indian Merchants and the Trade in the Indian Ocean').

16. Syed Ali Nawab and Charles Norman Seddon, trans., *Mirat-i-Ahmadi*, p. 117.

17. Claude Markovits, *Merchants, Traders, Entrepreneurs: Indian Business in the Colonial Era* (New Delhi: Permanent Black, 2008), pp. 196–200 (hereinafter cited as *Merchants, Traders, Entrepreneurs*).

18. Ashin Dasgupta, *Indian Merchants and the Decline of Surat,* pp. 20–21.

19. Lakshmi Subramanian, 'Capital and Crowd in a Declining Asian Port City: The Anglo-Bania Order and the Surat Riots of 1795', *Modern Asian Studies*, vol. 19, no. 2 (1985): p. 223.

20. Lakshmi Subramanian, 'Banias and the British: The Role of Indigenous Credit in the Process of Imperial Expansion in Western

India in the Second Half of the Eighteenth Century', *Modern Asian Studies*, vol. 21, no. 3 (1987): p. 476 (hereinafter cited as 'Banias and the British').

21. Ashin Dasgupta, 'Indian Merchants and the Trade in the Indian Ocean', p. 420.

22. Ashin Dasgupta, *Indian Merchants and the Decline of Surat*.

23. Harald Tambs-Lyche, *Power, Profit and Poetry: Traditional Society in Kathiawar* (New Delhi: Manohar Publishers, 1997), pp. 225–27, 251.

24. Douglas E. Haynes, *Rhetoric and Ritual in Colonial India: The Shaping of a Public Culture in Surat City, 1852–1928* (California: University of California Press, 1991), p. 38.

25. Petition of Lakmandas Jagannath Seth of the Banias and Waranasidas Jaidas Seth of the Shroffs for themselves and for all the Mahajans dated 22 August 1795, Public Department Diary of the Bombay Government (No. 114 A of 1795) (Maharashtra State Archives, Mumbai).

26. Ashin Dasgupta, *Indian Merchants and the Decline of Surat*, pp. 15–16.

27. Lakshmi Subramanian, *Indigenous Capital and Imperial Expansion*, pp. 22–45.

28. Ashin Dasgupta, *Indian Merchants and the Decline of Surat*, pp. 66ff, 73–74. *See* Holden Furber, *Bombay Presidency in the Mid-Eighteenth Century* (New York: Asia Publishing House, 1965), pp. 53–70.

29. Lakshmi Subramanian, *Indigenous Capital and Imperial Expansion*, pp. 82–100.

30. Ibid., pp. 80–100.

31. Amalendu Guha, 'More about Parsi Seths: Their Roots, Entrepreneurship and Comprador Role, 1650–1918', *Economic and Political Weekly,* vol. XIX, no. 3 (1984): pp. 117–32. *See* 'The Comprador Role of Parsi Seths, 1750–1830', *Economic and Political Weekly*, vol. V, no. 48 (1970): pp. 1933, 1935, 1938.

32. Howard Spodek, 'Rulers, Merchants and Other Groups in the City-States of Saurashtra, India Around 1800', *Comparative Studies in Society and History*, vol. 16, no. 4 (1974): pp. 448–70.

33. Lakshmi Subramanian, *Indigenous Capital and Imperial Expansion*, pp. 265–70.

34. Lakshmi Subramanian, 'Banias and the British', pp. 473–510. For a general understanding of the importance of merchant power *see* C.A. Bayly, *Rulers, Townsmen and Bazaars: North Indian Society in the Age of British Expansion, 1770–1870* (Cambridge: Cambridge University Press, 1983), pp. 169–183 (hereinafter cited as *Rulers, Townsmen and Bazaars*).

35. Geoffrey Parker, 'The Emergence of Modern Finance in Europe, 1500–1730' in *The Fontana Economic History of Europe, Volume 2, The Sixteenth and Seventeenth Centuries*, ed. Carlo M. Cipolla (Glasgow: Collins/Fontana Books, 1974), p. 527–94.

36. C.A. Bayly, *Rulers, Townsmen and Bazaars*, pp. 158–59.

37. Lakshmi Subramanian, 'Banias and the British', pp. 493–95.

38. Bernard S. Cohn, 'The Initial British Impact on India: A Case Study of the Benares Region', *The Journal of Asian Studies*, vol. 19, no. 4 (1960): p. 422.

39. John Malcolm, *A Memoir of Central India Including Malwa and Adjoining Provinces With the History, And Copious Illustrations, of the Past and Present Condition of That Country: Volume II* (London: Parbury, Allen & Co., 1823), p. 90.

40. Lakshmi Subramanian, 'Banias and the British', pp. 480, 486, 493–94.

41. C.A. Bayly, *Rulers, Townsmen and Bazaars,* pp. 234–37.

42. K.N. Chaudhuri, 'Foreign Trade and the Balance of Payments (1757–1947)' in *The Cambridge Economic History of India: Volume II,* eds Dharma Kumar and Meghnad Desai (New Delhi: Orient Longman, 1984), pp. 807–20 (hereinafter cited as 'Foreign Trade and the Balance of Payments').

43. Amales Tripathi, *Trade and Finance in the Bengal Presidency, 1793–1833* (New Delhi: OUP, 1979), pp. 1–11, 110–20.

44. B.R. Tomlinson, '"The Only Merchant in Calcutta": John Fergusson and the Growth of Private Trade in Bengal, 1775–1790' in *Africa, Empire and Globalization*, eds Toyin Falola and

Emily Brownell (North Carolina: Carolina Academic Press, 2011), pp. 237–51.

45. K.N. Chaudhuri, 'Foreign Trade and the Balance of Payments', pp. 805–35. *See* Asiya Siddiqi, *Trade and Finance in Colonial India, 1750–1860* (New Delhi: OUP, 1995), pp. 16–17ff.

46. Ibid.

47. Claude Markovits, *Merchants, Traders, Entrepreneurs*, p. 131.

48. Rajat Kanta Ray, 'Asian Capital in the Era of European Domination: The Rise of the Bazaar, 1800–1914', *Modern Asian Studies*, vol. 29, no. 3 (1995): pp. 449–554 (hereinafter cited as 'Asian Capital').

49. R.A. Wadia, *The Bombay Dockyard and the Wadia Master Builders* (Bombay: Privately published, 1955), pp. 40–43. *See* Introduction.

50. Dwijendra Tripathi, *The History of Indian Business*, pp. 103, 109.

51. D.E. Wacha, *A Financial Chapter in the History of Bombay City* (Bombay: A.J. Combridge and Co., 1910), p. 48.

52. Rajat Kanta Ray, 'Asian Capital', pp. 450–554. The article defines and describes the activities of the bazaar as a crucial mediating space between export operations and the production sector.

53. James Douglas, *A Book of Bombay* (Bombay: Gazette Steam Press, 1883), pp. 473–82.

54. Quoted in Lakshmi Subramanian and Rajat Kanta Ray, 'Merchants and Politics', p. 69.

2. Trawadi Arjunji Nathji: The 'Honourable Company's Shroff'

1. Michelguglielmo Torri, 'Trapped Inside the Colonial Order: The Hindu Bankers of Surat and Their Business World During the Second Half of the Eighteenth Century', *Modern Asian Studies*, vol. 25, no. 2 (1991): p. 374 (hereinafter cited as 'Trapped Inside the Colonial Order').

2. Ibid., p. 375.

3. James Douglas, *A Book of Bombay* (Bombay: Gazette Steam Press, 1883), p. 477 (hereinafter cited as *A Book of Bombay*).

4. Ashin Dasgupta, *Indian Merchants and the Decline of Surat: 1700–1750* (New Delhi: Manohar Publishers, 1994), pp. 199–239.

5. Lakshmi Subramanian, *Indigenous Capital and Imperial Expansion: Bombay, Surat and the West Coast* (New Delhi: OUP, 1996), pp. 83–96 (hereinafter cited as *Indigenous Capital and Imperial Expansion*).

6. Lakshmi Subramanian, 'Banias and the British: The Role of Indigenous Credit in the Process of Imperial Expansion in Western India in the Second-Half of the Eighteenth Century', *Modern Asian Studies*, vol. 21, no. 3 (1987): p. 484.

7. C.A. Bayly, *Rulers, Townsmen and Bazaars: North Indian Society in the Age of British Expansion, 1770–1870* (Cambridge: Cambridge University Press, 1983), pp. 127, 141, 156.

8. Case of Hiranand Tesbanvs Haribhai Bhaidas, Mayors Court Registers, 3 November 1789: p. 409ff (Maharashtra State Archives, Mumbai). Arjunji was asked to give evidence on the usage of a particular allowance referred to as 'vandanny' which was generally added to the receipt of the amount borrowed. The banker stated that many smaller shroffs were in the practice of charging this but that it was not practised by those of respectability.

9. 'Trapped Inside the Colonial Order', p. 377.

10. *Calendar of Persian Correspondence: 1788–89: Volume VIII (Calcutta and Delhi)* (New Delhi: National Archives of India, 1953), p. 157.

11. K.D. Bhargava, ed., *Calendar of Persian Correspondence: 1792–93: Volume X* (New Delhi: National Archives of India, 1959), p. 312.

12. Lakshmi Subramanian, *Indigenous Capital and Imperial Expansion*, pp. 157–59.

13. Ibid., p. 158.

14. Ibid., p. 188.

15. Home Public Consultations (Secretary to Government) dated 4 April 1789.

16. John Malcolm, *A Memoir of Central India Including Malwa and Adjoining Provinces With the History, and Copious Illustrations, of the Past and Present Condition of That Country: Volume II* (London: Parbury, Allen & Co., 1823), p. 89.

17. *Calendar of Persian Correspondence: 1794–95: Volume XI (Calcutta)* (New Delhi: National Archives of India, 1969), p. 184.

18. James Douglas, *A Book of Bombay*, p. 475–76. *See* Lakshmi Subramanian, *Indigenous Capital and Imperial Expansion*, pp. 299–305.

19. For details of the negotiations and the bankers' manoeuvring tactics *see* Lakshmi Subramanian, 'Arms and the Merchant: The Making of the Bania Raj in Late Eighteenth-Century India', *South Asia*, vol. XXIV, no. 2 (2001): p. 1–27 (hereinafter cited as 'Arms and the Merchant').

20. Ibid., pp. 18–19.

21. The details of the contract and the negotiations that ensued over its terms and interpretation are based on a close examination of the Surat Factory Diaries (1759–1808) (Maharashtra State Archives, Mumbai) and the Boards Collection F/4/269 (5907–59, vol. 269, Bombay Military Consultation). For full details *see* Lakshmi Subramanian, 'Arms and the Merchant'.

22. Ibid., p.18. For details of the contract *see* the Surat Factory Diary (No. 45 of 1806); and Council Meeting dated 12 January 1806, p. 32. For letter and enclosures from Bombay that included a report from the Assistant-Collector of Surat on the definitions of hundi conventions *see* letter from Trawadi to Governor Duncan, p. 397ff (Maharashtra State Archives, Mumbai).

23. Surat Factory Diary (No. 43 of 1804), p. 240. For Arjunji's comments on the contract *see* letter to Arjunji dated 16 September 1803, p. 242, and request of Arjunji dated 29 August 1804, pp. 340ff (Maharashtra State Archives, Mumbai).

24. Lakshmi Subramanian, 'Arms and the Merchant', p. 19.

25. Ibid., p. 22.

26. Ibid., p. 21.

27. Surat Factory Diary (No. 45 of 1806); and letter from Arjunji to Governor Duncan dated 8 January 1806, p. 35. *See* Boards Collections, vol. 269, extract from the Bombay Military Consultations, F/4/269 (5907–5918) (Maharashtra State Archives, Mumbai).

28. For a fuller analysis of the trial of 1800 *see* Lakshmi Subramanian, 'A Trial in Transition: Courts, Merchants and Identities in Western India, circa 1800', *Indian Economic and Social History Review,* vol. 41, no. 3 (2004): pp. 269–82 (hereinafter cited as 'A Trial in Transition').

29. This section of the narrative draws heavily from my earlier work that analysed this case in some detail. *See* Lakshmi Subramanian, 'A Trial in Transition'. This curious case was the subject of extensive discussion among the Surat Council of the Company.

30. *See* Lakshmi Subramanian, 'A Trial in Transition'.

31. Surat Factory Diary (No. 51 (Part 1) of 1800); and letter from Ramsay dated 13 December 1800 (Maharashtra State Archives, Mumbai).

32. Lakshmi Subramanian, 'A Trial in Transition', p. 284.

33. Ibid., p. 287.

34. Ibid.

35. Douglas E. Haynes, *Rhetoric and Ritual in Colonial India: The Shaping of a Public Culture in Surat City, 1852–1928* (New Delhi: OUP, 1992), pp. 52–68.

36. Thomas Timberg, 'Three Types of the Marwari Firm', *Indian Economic and Social Review*, vol. 10, no. 3 (1973): pp. 1–36.

37. Surat Factory Diary (No. 47 of 1808); and petition of Trawadi's gomasta dated 14 February 1808 and government's letter dated 23 February 1808 (Maharashtra State Archives, Mumbai).

38. James Douglas, *A Book of Bombay*, pp. 473–82.

3. Jamsetjee Jeejeebhoy: The First Parsi Baronet

1. Claude Markovits, *Merchants, Traders, Entrepreneurs: Indian Business in the Colonial Era* (New Delhi: Permanent Black, 2008), pp. 129, 141–47 (hereinafter cited as *Merchants, Traders, Entrepreneurs*).

2. Deirdre N. McCloskey, *Bourgeois Dignity: Why Economics Cannot Explain the Modern World* (Chicago: University of Chicago Press, 2010), pp. 10–19, 22–30.

3. David L. White, *Competition and Collaboration: Parsi Merchants and the English East India Company in 18ᵗʰ Century India* (New Delhi: Manohar Publishers, 1995), pp. 63–78 (hereinafter cited as *Competition and Collaboration*).

4. M.D. David, *History of Bombay, 1661–1708* (Bombay: University of Bombay, 1973). *See* S.M. Edwardes, ed., *Gazetteer of Bombay City and Island* (Bombay: Time Press, 1909). Both these works are reference works and give detailed descriptions of the city, its early history, fortifications and inhabitants.

5. Amar Farooqi, *Opium City: The Making of Early Victorian Bombay* (Gurgaon: Three Essays Collective, 2006), pp. 6–7 (hereinafter cited as *Opium City*); and Lakshmi Subramanian, *Indigenous Capital and Imperial Expansion: Bombay, Surat and the West Coast* (New Delhi: OUP, 1996), pp. 75–76 (hereinafter cited as *Indigenous Capital and Imperial Expansion*).

6. Lakshmi Subramanian, *Indigenous Capital and Imperial Expansion*, pp. 75–100.

7. Amalendu Guha, 'More About the Parsi Seths: Their Roots, Entrepreneurship and Comprador Role, 1650–1918' in *Business Communities of India: A Historical Perspective,* ed. Dwijendra Tripathi (New Delhi: Manohar Publishers, 1984), pp. 115–16.

8. Ashok V. Desai, 'The Origins of Parsi Enterprise', *Indian Economic and Social History Review*, vol. 5 (1968): pp. 307–17.

9. David L. White, *Competition and Collaboration,* pp. 38–39, 63–69, 78–79ff.

10. Cooverjee Sorabjee Nazir, The First Parsee Baronet (Bombay: Union Press, 1866), p. 6 (hereinafter cited as *The First Parsee Baronet*). The bottle business was apparently a lucrative one.

11. John Hinnells and Alan Williams, eds, *Parsis in India and the Diaspora* (England: Routledge, 2008), p. 123.

12. Pamela Nightingale, *Trade and Empire in Western India: 1784–1806* (Cambridge: Cambridge University Press, 1970), pp. 22–23, 46 (hereinafter cited as *Trade and Empire in Western India*).

13. Lakshmi Subramanian, *Indigenous Capital and Imperial Expansion*, pp. 7–9.

14. *See* Report of the Committee constituted by William Loper and D.C. Ramsey on the outlines of textile manufacture dated 24 December 1795. Commercial Department Diary of the Bombay Government (No. 12 of 1796), pp. 17ff (Maharashtra State Archives, Mumbai).

15. Asiya Siddiqi, 'The Business World of Jamsetjee Jeejeebhoy' in *Trade and Finance in Colonial India, 1750–1860*, ed. Asiya Siddiqi (New Delhi: OUP, 1995), pp. 186–217 (hereinafter cited as *Trade and Finance in Colonial India*).

16. Ibid., pp. 31–32.

17. Lakshmi Subramanian, 'Seths and Sahibs: Negotiated Relationships Between Indigenous Capital and the East India Company' in *Britain's Oceanic Empire Atlantic and Indian Ocean Worlds c. 1550–1850*, eds H.V. Bowen, Elizabeth Mancke, and John G. Reid (Cambridge: Cambridge University Press, 2012), pp. 323–32.

18. Lakshmi Subramanian, 'Reaping the Risks of Transition: Merchants and Trade in Western India c. 1750–1818' in *The Trading World of the Indian Ocean, 1500–1800*, ed. Om Prakash (New Delhi: Pearson Publications, 2012), pp. 285–309.

19. Alain Le Pichon, *China Trade and Empire: Jardine Matheson and Company and the Origins of British Rule in Hong Kong, 1827–43* (London: OUP, 2006), p. 6ff (hereinafter cited as *China Trade and Empire*).

20. Ibid., p. 7 (for lists of agency houses). *See* Amales Tripathi, *Trade and Finance in the Bengal Presidency, 1793–1833* (New Delhi: OUP, 1979), pp. 1–11.

21. Asiya Siddiqi, 'The Business World of Jamsetjee Jeejeebhoy', *Indian Economic and Social History Review*, vol. 19, nos. 3–4 (1982): p. 202 (hereinafter cited as 'The Business World of Jamsetjee Jeejeebhoy').

22. Pamela Nightingale, *Trade and Empire in Western India*, pp. 128–64.

23. Amalendu Guha, 'More about Parsi Seths: Their Roots,

Entrepreneurship and Comprador Role, 1650–1918', *Economic and Political Weekly*, vol. XIX, no. 3 (1984): pp. 117–32.

24. Asiya Siddiqi, 'The Business World of Jamsetjee Jeejeebhoy', pp. 187–218. *See* Claude Markovits, *Merchants, Traders, Entrepreneurs*, pp. 141–49.

25. Claude Markovits, *Merchants, Traders, Entrepreneurs*, p. 131; Amar Farooqi, *Opium City*, p. 9; and H.V. Bowen, 'The Integration of the Asian Textile Industry: Trade, Empire and British Exports of Raw Cotton from India to China during the Late Eighteenth and Early Nineteenth Centuries', pp. 11–17. Available online at: (http://www2.lse.ac.uk/economicHistory/Research/GEHN/HELSINKIBowen.pdf) (hereinafter cited as 'The Integration of the Asian Textile Industry').

26. Quoted in Ranbir Vohra, *The Making of India: A Historical Survey* (New York: M.E. Sharpe Inc., 2001), p. 63.

27. H.V. Bowen, 'The Integration of the Asian Textile Industry', p. 11.

28. Amar Farooqi, 'Opium Enterprise and Colonial Intervention in Malwa and Western India, 1800–1824', *Indian Economic and Social History Review*, vol. 32, no.4 (1995): pp. 462–65 (hereinafter cited as 'Opium Enterprise and Colonial Intervention in Malwa and Western India').

29. Alain Le Pichon, *China Trade and Empire*, pp. 3–12, 18–27. *See* Maggie Keswick, ed., *The Thistle and the Jade: A Celebration of 175 Years of Jardine Matheson* (London: Frances Lincoln Limited, 1982), pp. 20–27 (hereinafter cited as *The Thistle and the Jade*).

30. Ibid., p. 22.

31. Amar Farooqi, 'Opium Enterprise and Colonial Intervention in Malwa and Western India', pp. 450–67.

32. For a tabular representation of opium imports into China from Malwa *see* Elijah Coleman Bridgman, Samuel Wells, eds, *The Chinese Repository: Volume 6: May 1837 to April 1838* (Canton: Printed for the proprietors, 1838), p. 196.

33. Amar Farooqi, *Opium City*, pp. 33–34.

34. D.F. Karaka, *History of the Parsis Including their Manners, Customs, Religion and Present Position: Volume II* (London: Macmillan and Co., 1884), p. 57.

35. Amar Farooqi, *Opium City*, pp. 33–34.

36. Cooverjee Sorabjee Nazir, *The First Parsee Baronet*, pp. 13, 14, 18–23.

37. Dwijendra Tripathi, *The Oxford History of Indian Business* (New Delhi: OUP, 2004), p. 82 (hereinafter cited as *The History of Indian Business*).

38. Maggie Keswick, ed., *The Thistle and the Jade,* pp. 20–21.

39. Anne Bulley, *The Bombay Country Ships, 1790–1833* (Great Britain: Curzon Press, 2000), pp. 153–62.

40. Cooverjee Sorabjee Nazir, *The First Parsee Baronet*, p. 28.

41. Asiya Siddiqi, *Trade and Finance in Colonial India,* p. 195.

42. Dwijendra Tripathi, *The History of Indian Business*, p. 82.

43. Diaries of Sir Jamsetjee Jeejeebhoy (Acc. No. 359), letter to Jardine Matheson dated 11 August 1849, University Library, Mumbai.

44. Jardine Matheson Papers (Acc. No. 2190), letter dated 25 May 1831 from Jamsetjee Jeejeebhoy to Magniac and Company (B6/4/2034–2394), University of Cambridge.

45. Ibid.

46. Ibid.

47. Diaries of Sir Jamsetjee Jeejeebhoy (Acc. No. 354), letter dated 12 February 1845, University Library, Mumbai.

48. Jardine Matheson Papers (Acc. No. 1008), letter to Magniac and Company dated 17 March 1829, University of Cambridge Library.

49. Jardine Matheson Papers (Acc. Nos. 1042 and 1043), University of Cambridge Library.

50. Diaries of Sir Jamsetjee Jeejeebhoy (Acc. No. 359), letter to Jardine Matheson dated 3 September 1849, University Library, Mumbai.

51. Asiya Siddiqi, 'The Business World of Jamsetjee Jeejeebhoy', p. 203.

52. Diaries of Sir Jamsetjee Jeejeebhoy (Acc. No. 359), letter to Jardine Matheson dated 16 December 1849, University Library, Mumbai.

53. Asiya Siddiqi, 'The Business World of Jamsetjee Jeejeebhoy', pp. 203–208, 212–216.

54. Quoted in Asiya Siddiqi, *Trade and Finance in Colonial India*, p. 213.

55. Ibid., p. 212, 214.

56. Ibid., p. 214.

57. Jardine Matheson Papers (Acc. No. 2805) (B6/4/2624–2829). The letter from Cursetjee Ardaser to Magniac stated 'The Marwarees at Malwa say that owing to large duties here they never intended to bring much of their opium to Bombay but will try to carry it to Daman more than last year.'

58. George Buist, 'Sir Jamsetjee Jeejeebhoy: A Parsee Merchant', *The North American Review*, vol. 73, no. 152 (1851): p. 139 (hereinafter cited as 'A Parsee Merchant').

59. Ibid.

60. Jesse S. Palsetia, *The Parsis of India: Preservation of Identity in Bombay City* (The Netherlands: Brill, 2001), pp. 128–37. According to Palsetia, Parsi charity assumed political dimensions under a colonial regime.

61. General Department (No. 50 of 1848) (Maharashtra State Archives, Mumbai).

62. Jesse S. Palsetia, 'Merchant Charity and Public Identity Formation in Colonial India: The Case of Jamsetjee Jeejeebhoy', *Journal of Asian and African Studies*, vol. 40, no. 3 (2005): pp. 197–207.

63. George Buist, 'A Parsee Merchant', p. 135.

64. Preeti Chopra, 'A Joint Enterprise: The Creation of a New Landscape in British Bombay, (1839–1918)', *Governance, Mumbai Readers 2010: Urban Design Research Institute* (2011). Available online at: http://www.udri.org/udriMumbaiReader10/20%20Preeti%20Chopra%20-%20A%20Joint%20Enterprise,%20The%20Creation%20of%20a%20New%20Landscape%20in%

20British%20Bombay%20(1839-1918).pdf? phpMyAdmin= w6qdoDhnTY-UA44T6XZMtfF7FTd. Chopra demonstrates how early philanthropic activity in Bombay city was concerned with space and municipal improvements. She also maintains that the making of Bombay city as a space was a joint enterprise.

65. George Buist, 'A Parsee Merchant', p. 137.

66. Delphine Menant, 'Zoroastrianism and the Parsis' in *Great Religions of the World*, ed. Herbert A. Giles (London: Harper and Brothers Publishers, 1901), p. 116.

67. Christine Dobbin, 'The Parsi Panchayat in Bombay City in the Nineteenth Century', *Modern Asian Studies*, vol. 4, no. 2 (1970): pp. 149–64.

68. Ibid.

69. Ibid., pp. 157–58.

70. Letters of Sir Jamsetjee Jeejeebhoy (Acc. No. 359), letter to Charles Forbes dated 11 January 1849, University Library, Mumbai.

71. Ibid., p. 71, letter dated 14 March 1849.

72. Ibid., p.73, letter dated 14 March 1849.

73. Diaries of Sir Jamsetjee Jeejeebhoy (Acc. No. 354), letter dated 29 January 1845, University Library, Mumbai.

74. George Buist, 'A Parsee Merchant', p. 142.

75. D.F. Karaka, *A History of the Parsis: Volume II* (London: Macmillan & Co., 1884), p. 104. Karaka actually mentions every single charity Jamsetjee extended and the various tributes that were paid to him on the occasion of his knighthood.

76. *See* issue of *The Bombay Courier* dated 4 June 1842, vol. 15, no. 32 (9 August 1842). Available at: http://www.houghton.idv.hk/.

77. Edition of *Friends of China* dated 22 December 1842, p. 104. Available at: http://www.houghton.idv.hk/.

78. *See* the eulogy of the editor of *The Canton Register,* to James Matheson dated 15 March 1842, vol. 15, no. 11. Available at: http://www.houghton.idv.hk/.

4. Premchand Roychand: A Man for All Seasons

1. D.E. Wacha, *Premchund Roychund: His Early Life and Career* (Bombay: The Times Press, 1913), pp. 1–233 (hereinafter cited as *Premchund Roychund: His Early Life and Career*); and Sharada Dwivedi, *Premchand Roychand (1831–1906): His Life and Times* (Mumbai: Eminence Designs Pvt. Ltd, 2006), pp. 1–112 (hereinafter cited as *Premchand Roychand: His Life and Times*) Wacha's account is probably the most detailed and near-contemporary account we have of Premchand Roychand.
2. Amiya Bagchi, *The Evolution of the State Bank of India: Volume I—The Roots, 1806–1860* (New Delhi: Penguin Books India, 2006), pp. 906–29) (hereinafter cited as *The Evolution of the State Bank*).
3. Rajat K. Ray, *Entrepreneurship and Industry in India: Themes in Indian History* (New Delhi: OUP, 1992), p. 41 (hereinafter cited as *Entrepreneurship and Industry in India*).
4. For details of Premchand Roychand's life and career *see* D.E. Wacha, *Premchund Roychund: His Early Life and Career*, pp. 12–15. My narrative draws largely from Wacha's account.
5. D.E. Wacha, *Shells from the Sands of Bombay; Being My Recollections and Reminiscences, 1860–1875* (Bombay: Indian Newspaper Co. Ltd, 1920), pp. 102–04.
6. Dwijendra Tripathi, *The Oxford History of Indian Business* (New Delhi: OUP, 2004) (hereinafter cited as *The History of Indian Business*), p. 102.
7. Mridula Ramanna, 'Social Background of the Educated in Bombay City: 1824–1858', Economic and Political Weekly, vol. 24, no. 4 (1989): pp. 203–11. *See* Sharada Dwivedi, *Premchand Roychand: His Life and Times*, p. 14.
8. Dwijendra Tripathi, *The History of Indian Business*, p. 103.
9. D.E. Wacha, *Premchund Roychund: His Early Life and Career*, pp. 15–21. *See* Sharada Dwivedi, *Premchand Roychand: His Life and Times*, p. 39.
10. Amiya Bagchi, *The Evolution of the State Bank*, p. 441–42.

11. Ibid., p. 451.
12. D.E. Wacha, *Premchund Roychund: His Early Life and Career*, pp. 39–43.
13. Lakshmi Subramanian, *Indigenous Capital and Imperial Expansion: Bombay, Surat and the West Coast* (New Delhi: OUP, 1996), pp. 204–06.
14. Lakshmi Subramanian, 'Banias and the British: The Role of Indigenous Credit in the Process of Imperial Expansion in Western India in the Second Half of the Eighteenth Century', *Modern Asian Studies*, vol. 21, no. 3 (1987): pp. 502–04.
15. Sharada Dwivedi, *Premchand Roychand: His Life and Times*, p. 19.
16. Rajat K. Ray, *Entrepreneurship and Industry in India*, p. 23.
17. Amiya Bagchi, 'Transition from Indian to British Indian Systems of Money and Banking, 1800–1850', *Modern Asian Studies*, vol. 19, no. 3 (1985): pp. 508–09, 511.
18. *See* the issue of *The Bombay Courier* dated 19 September 1845 (Maharashtra State Archives, Mumbai).
19. Amiya Bagchi, *The Evolution of the State Bank*, pp. 912–13.
20. D.E. Wacha, *Premchund Roychund: His Early Life and Career*, pp. 40–43.
21. Dwijendra Tripathi, *The History of Indian Business*, p. 103.
22. Sharada Dwivedi, *Premchand Roychand: His Life and Times*, p. 25.
23. Dwijendra Tripathi, *The History of Indian Business*, pp. 100–02.
24. Sharada Dwivedi, *Premchand Roychand: His Life and Times*, p. 21.
25. D.E. Wacha, *Premchund Roychund: His Early Life and Career*, pp. 55–56.
26. D.E. Wacha, *A Financial Chapter in the History of Bombay* (Bombay: A.J. Combridge & Co., 1910, p. 11 (hereinafter cited as *A Financial Chapter in the History of Bombay*).
27. *See* the issue of *Bombay Gazette* (January–June 1862) (Maharashtra State Archives, Mumbai).
28. D.E. Wacha, *Premchund Roychund: His Early Life and Career*, p. 17. *See* Bagchi, *The Evolution of the State Bank*, p. 733.
29. For export and import figures *see* D.E. Wacha, *A Financial Chapter in the History of Bombay*, p. 15.

30. D.E. Wacha, *Premchund Roychund: His Early Life and Career*, p. 43.

31. Amiya Bagchi, *The Evolution of the State Bank*, p. 917.

32. Ibid., p. 900.

33. Ibid., pp. 908–09.

34. Preeti Chopra, 'A Joint Enterprise: The Creation of a New Landscape in British Bombay, (1839–1918)', *Governance, Mumbai Readers 2010: Urban Design Research Institute* (2011). Available online at:http://www.udri.org/udri/MumbaiReader10/20%20Preeti%20Chopra%20-%20A%20Joint%20Enterprise,%20The%20Creation%20of%20a%20New%20Landscape%20in%20British%20Bombay%20(1839-1918).pdf?phpMyAdmin=w6qdoDhnTY-UA44T6XZMtfF7FTd (hereinafter cited as 'A Joint Enterprise').

35. Mariam Dossal, *Imperial Designs and Indian Realities: The Planning of Bombay City, 1845–1875* (Bombay: OUP, 1991), pp. 150, 152, 153ff (hereinafter cited as *Imperial Designs and Indian Realities*).

36. Amiya Bagchi, *The Evolution of the State Bank*, p. 898.

37. Quoted in Mariam Dossal, *Imperial Designs and Indian Realities*, p. 153.

38. Raymond Sullivan, *One Hundred Years of Bombay* (Bombay: Times of India Press, 1937), p. 69 (hereinafter cited as *One Hundred Years of Bombay*).

39. D.E. Wacha, *A Financial Chapter in the History of Bombay*, pp. 54–55. *See* Amiya Bagchi, *The Evolution of the State Bank*, p. 914.

40. D.E. Wacha, *A Financial Chapter in the History of Bombay*, p. 34.

41. Amiya Bagchi, *The Evolution of the State Bank*, p. 913.

42. D.E. Wacha, A *Financial Chapter in the History of Bombay*, p. 39.

43. Quoted in Mariam Dossal, *Imperial Designs and Indian Realities*, p. 161.

44. *Report of the Royal Commission on the Old Bank of Bombay* (Bombay: Bombay Gazette Press, 1869) p. 8, (hereinafter cited as *Report of the Bombay Bank Commission*).

45. Amiya Bagchi, *The Evolution of the State Bank*, pp. 910–12.

46. Ibid., p. 911.

47. Quoted in Dwijendra Tripathi, *The History of Indian Business*, p. 102. *See* D.E. Wacha, *Premchund Roychund: His Early Life and Career*, pp. 55–56.

48. D.E. Wacha, *Premchund Roychund: His Early Life and Career*, p. 56.

49. Amiya Bagchi. *The Evolution of the State Bank*, p. 907–08.

50. *Report of the Bombay Bank Commission*, pp. 13–14.

51. Ibid., p. 9.

52. Ibid., p. 12.

53. Diaries of Jamsetjee Jeejeebhoy (Acc. No. 387), letter to William Ramsay dated 23 June 1865, University Library, Mumbai.

54. Dwijendra Tripathi, *The History of Indian Business*, p. 104.

55. Ibid. *See* D.E. Wacha, *A Financial Chapter in the History of Bombay*, pp. 67–76.

56. Dwijendra Tripathi, *The History of Indian Business*, p. 104.

57. Raymond Sullivan, *One Hundred Years of Bombay*, p. 73ff.

58. Diaries of Jamsetjee Jeejeebhoy (Acc. No. 387), letter to William Ramsey dated 23 June 1865, University Library, Mumbai.

59. Raymond Sullivan, *One Hundred Years of Bombay*, p. 74.

60. D.E. Wacha, *A Financial Chapter in the History of Bombay*, p. 59.

61. *Report of the Bombay Bank Commission*, pp. 10–11.

62. D.E. Wacha, *Premchund Roychund: His Early Life and Career*, p. 191.

63. Sharada Dwivedi, *Premchand Roychand: His Life and Times*, p. 53.

64. Jesse S. Palsetia, *The Parsis of India: Preservation of Identity in Bombay City* (The Netherlands: Brill, 2001). The author makes a strong case for the public activities of the community and its close intersection with early identity politics.

65. *See* extract from the proceedings of the Government of Bombay dated 26 January 1865, General Department (No. 30 of 1865) (Maharashtra State Archives, Mumbai).

66. D.E. Wacha, *Premchund Roychund: His Early Life and Career*, p. 87.

67. Asiya Siddiqi, 'The Business World of Jamsetjee Jeejeebhoy' in *Trade and Finance in Colonial India, 1750–1860*, ed. Asiya Siddiqi (New Delhi: OUP, 1995), p. 192.

68. Preeti Chopra, 'A Joint Enterprise', p. 336.

69. Mariam Dossall, *Imperial Designs and Indian Realities*, p. 96–124ff.
70. Preeti Chopra, 'A Joint Enterprise', p. 337.

Epilogue: The Romance of Commerce

1. Lakshmi Subramanian and Rajat Kanta Ray, 'Merchants and Politics From the Great Mughal to the East India Company' in *Business and Politics in India: A Historical Perspective*, ed. Dwijendra Tripathi (New Delhi: Manohar Publishers, 1991), p. 67 (hereinafter cited as 'Merchants and Politics').
2. Diaries of Jamsetjee Jeejeebhoy (Acc. No. 369), letter dated 26 March 1842, University Library, Mumbai.
3. C.A. Bayly, *Rulers, Townsmen and Bazaars: North Indian Society in the Age of British Expansion, 1770–1870* (Cambridge: Cambridge University Press, 1983) pp. 169–83; and Lakshmi Subramanian, *Indigenous Capital and Imperial Expansion: Bombay, Surat and the West Coast* (New Delhi: OUP, 1996), pp. 317–39.
4. Dwijendra Tripathi, quoted in Lakshmi Subramanian and Rajat Kanta Ray, 'Merchants and Politics', p. 67.
5. Diaries of Jamsetjee Jeejeebhoy (Acc. No. 369), letter dated 30 April 1942, University Library, Mumbai.
6. Claude Markovits, *Merchants, Traders, Entrepreneurs: Indian Business in the Colonial Era* (New Delhi: Permanent Black, 2008), pp. 187–220.
7. Ibid., pp. 196–202.
8. Quoted in Amalendu Guha, 'More About the Parsi Seths: Their Roots, Entrepreneurship and Comprador Role, 1650–1918' in *Business Communities of India: A Historical Perspective*, ed. Dwijendra Tripathi (New Delhi: Manohar Publishers, 1984), p. 143.
9. Ibid., p. 140.
10. Gaurav Desai, 'Commerce as Romance: Nanji Kalidas Mehta's Dream Half-Expressed', *Research in African Literatures*, vol. 42, no. 3 (2011): pp. 147–65.

BIBLIOGRAPHY

This is a select bibliography. I list here only the writings that have been of use in the making of this book. This list is by no means a complete record of all the works and sources I have consulted. It indicates some key texts and primary archival resources, and the substance and range of reading upon which I have formed my ideas, and I intend it to serve as a convenience for those who wish to pursue the study of or generally peruse the historical accounts and narratives underlining colonial Bombay.

Archival and Printed Sources

Public Department Diary of the Bombay Government (1740–1808). Maharashtra State Archives, Mumbai.

Surat Factory Diary (1759–1808). Maharashtra State Archives, Mumbai.

General Department Diary of the Bombay Government (No. 30 of 1865).

Diaries of Jamsetjee Jeejeebhoy (1/2/1826–29/12/1876). Bombay University Library.

The Bombay Bank Commission Report on the Royal Commission on the Old Bank of Bombay: Bombay Gazette Press, 1869.

Books and Articles

Alam, Muzaffar. *The Crisis of Empire in Mughal North India: Awadh and the Punjab, 1707–1748*. New Delhi: OUP, 1986.

Bagchi, Amiya. *The Evolution of the State Bank of India: Volume I—The Roots, 1806–1876*. Bombay: OUP, 1987.

Bayly, C.A. *Rulers, Townsmen and Bazaars: North Indian Society in the Age of British Expansion 1770–1870*. Cambridge: Cambridge University Press, 1983.

Bowen, H.V. *The Business of Empire: The East India Company and Imperial Britain, 1756–1833*. Cambridge: Cambridge University Press, 2006.

Chopra, Preeti. *A Joint Enterprise: The Creation of a New Landscape in British Bombay (1839–1918)*. Minnesota: University of Minnesota Press, 2011.

Dasgupta, Ashin. *Indian Merchants and the Decline of Surat: 1700–1750*. New Delhi: Manohar Publishers, 1994.

David, M.D. *History of Bombay, 1661–1708*. Bombay: University of Bombay, 1973.

Desai, Gaurav. 'Commerce as Romance: Nanji Kalidas Mehta's Dream Half-Expressed.' *Research in African Literatures*. Vol. 42, no. 3 (2011).

Dossal, Mariam. *Imperial Design and Indian Realities: The Planning of Bombay City, 1845–1875*. Bombay: OUP, 1991.

Douglas, James. *A Book of Bombay*. Bombay: Gazette Steam Press, 1883.

———*Bombay and Western India: A Series of Stray Papers*. London: S. Low, Marston & Company, 1893.

Dwivedi, Sharada. *Premchand Roychand (1831–1906): His Life and Times*. Mumbai: Eminence Designs Pvt. Ltd, 2006.

Farooqi, Amar. 'Opium Enterprise and Colonial Intervention in Malwa and Western India, 1800–1824.' *Indian Economic and Social History Review*. Vol. 32, no. 4 (1995).

———*Opium City: The Making of Early Victorian Bombay*. Gurgaon: Three Essays Collective, 2006.

Furber, Holden. *Bombay Presidency in the Mid-Eighteenth Century*. Bombay: Asia Publishing House, 1965.

Gordon, Stewart. *The Marathas: 1600–1818, The New Cambridge History of India*. Cambridge: Cambridge University Press, 1993.

Haynes, Douglas. *Rhetoric and Ritual in Colonial India: The Shaping of a Public Culture in Surat City, 1852–1928*. California: University of California, 1991.

Keswick, Maggie, ed. *The Thistle and the Jade: A Celebration of 175 Years of Jardine Matheson*. London: Frances Lincoln Limited, 1982.

Kumar, Dharma and Desai, Meghnad, eds, *The Cambridge Economic History of India: Volume II*. Cambridge: Cambridge University Press, 1983.

Malcolm, John. *A Memoir of Central India Including Malwa and Adjoining Provinces With The History, And Copious Illustrations, Of The Past and Present Condition of That Country*. London: Parbury, Allen & Co., 1823

Markovits, Claude. *Merchants, Traders, Entrepreneurs: Indian Business in the Colonial Era*. New Delhi: Permanent Black, 2008.

Marshall, Peter. *East Indian Fortunes: The British in Bengal in the Eighteenth Century*. Oxford: Clarendon Press, 1976.

Mukund, Kanakalatha. *The View from Below: Indigenous Society, Temples and the Early Colonial State in Tamilnadu, 1700–1835*. New Delhi: Orient Blackswan, 2005.

Natesan, G. *Famous Parsis: Biographical and Critical Sketches of Patriots, Philanthropists, Politicians, Reformers, Scholars and Captains of Industry*. Madras: A. Natesan & Co., 1930.

Nazir, Cooverjee Sorabjee. *The First Parsee Baronet* (Bombay: Union Press, 1866).

Nightingale, Pamela. *Trade and Empire in Western India: 1784–1806*. Cambridge: Cambridge University Press, 1970.

Palsetia, Jesse S. *The Parsis of India: Preservation of Identity in Bombay City*. The Netherlands: Brill, 2001.

Pichon, Alain Le. *China Trade and Empire: Jardine Matheson and Company and the Origins of British Rule in Hong Kong, 1827–43*. London: OUP, 2006.

Ray, Rajat Kanta, ed. *Entrepreneurship and Industry in India: 1800–1947*. New Delhi: OUP, 1992.

Roy, Tirthankar. *The Economic History of India: 1857–1947*. New Delhi: OUP, 2000.

Siddiqi, Asiya, ed. *Trade and Finance in Colonial India, 1750–1860.* New Delhi: OUP, 1995

Subramanian, Lakshmi. *Indigenous Capital and Imperial Expansion: Bombay, Surat and the West Coast.* New Delhi: OUP, 1996.

Sullivan, Raymond. *One Hundred Years of Bombay.* Bombay: Times of India Press, 1937.

Timberg, Thomas A. *The Marwaris, From Traders to Industrialists.* New Delhi: Vikas Publishing House, 1977.

Torri, Michelguglielmo. 'Trapped Inside the Colonial Order: The Hindu Bankers of Surat and Their Business World During the Second Half of the Eighteenth Century'. *Modern Asian Studies.* Vol. 25, no. 2 (1991).

Tripathi, Amales. *Trade and Finance in the Bengal Presidency, 1793–1833.* New Delhi: OUP, 1979.

Tripathi, Dwijendra, ed. *Business and Politics in India: A Historical Perspective.* New Delhi: Manohar Publishers, 1991.

———*The Dynamics of a Tradition: Kasturbhai Lalbhai and His Entrepreneurship. New* Delhi: Manohar Publishers, 1981.

———*The Oxford History of Indian Business.* New Delhi: OUP, 2004.

Wacha, D.E. *Premchund Roychund: His Early Life and Career.* Bombay: The Times Press, 1913.

———*Shells From the Sands of Bombay; Being My Recollections and Reminiscences, 1860–1875.* Bombay: Indian Newspaper Co. Ltd, 1920.

White, David L. *Competition and Collaboration: Parsi Merchants and the English East India Company in 18th Century India.* New Delhi: Manohar Publishers, 1995.